He Who Laughs Lasts

He Who Laughs Lasts

Shawn Lovley

Writers Club Press
San Jose New York Lincoln Shanghai

He Who Laughs Lasts

All Rights Reserved © 2001 by Shawn Lovley

No part of this book may be reproduced or transmitted in any form or by any means, graphic, electronic, or mechanical, including photocopying, recording, taping, or by any information storage retrieval system, without the permission in writing from the publisher.

Writers Club Press
an imprint of iUniverse.com, Inc.

For information address:
iUniverse.com, Inc.
5220 S 16th, Ste. 200
Lincoln, NE 68512
www.iuniverse.com

ISBN: 0-595-15652-5

Printed in the United States of America

Dedication

◆

To the memory of my father, whose love and
laughter have helped me last.

Contents

Dedication v
Foreword ix
Acknowledgements xiii
Just Joking?—An Introduction 1
Holy Cow! 4
School Daze 17
Oh, You Animal! 29
Food Fight! 40
Gender Benders 53
Just For The Health Of It 64
Say What? 76
Color Me ~~Blue~~ Blonde 86
Live and Laugh 101
~~Tea~~ Time 114
The Technodunce 125
Take My WordPlay For It 138
Work Weirdness 150
About the Author 163

Foreword

by
Bernie Siegel, M.D.

Love and laughter are required to build and hold our lives together. For me love makes up the bricks which we build with. Ask yourself what you are capable of loving and you will know what your life is about. But what holds that life and the bricks together? We need mortar—and the mortar of life is humor. For me, this represents childlike humor that isn't offensive and doesn't hurt or upset anyone. Humor of this type heals lives. He Who **Laughs Lasts** is filled with healing humor and is a joy to read.

One of the things that convinced me of the value of humor occurred one evening when my wife and I were out lecturing. My wife Bobbie does stand-up one-liner comedy as part of our presentation so people can feel the benefit of laughter and not just hear a lecture about how it alters our physiology. On this particular evening I did not take her seat in the audience, as I usually do, because of the set-up of the stage. I sat behind her and watched the audience.

The change in their physical appearance after laughing for 15-20 minutes was striking, and made me a firm believer in the benefits of humor. Two of her straight lines are "He who laughs lasts" and "Laughter is contagious. Be a carrier." I agree.

On a personal level, what I mean by childlike humor is seeing the world through a child's eyes. If you see a sign saying 'Wet Floor,' go ahead and do it. On airline flights I often came out of the lavatory looking worried and said "I may have damaged the plane." Attendants would hurry over and I'd say "I dropped something from Italy in the toilet and then I saw the sign that said not to throw foreign objects in the toilet." Now all the planes have signs that say things like "Don't throw solid objects in the toilet" because of crazy people like me.

Many years ago I fell off our roof when a ladder I was climbing broke. Later, I told the audience I was relating the story to that I must have an angel, because I landed on my feet, which seemed physically impossible considering the angle of the ladder and so on. A man came up at the end of my talk and said, "You do have an angel and I know his name." I said "how do you know his name?" "What did you say when the ladder broke?" he asked. "Oh Shit!" I admitted, to which he said "That's your angel's name." I laughed, but didn't realize what a gift he had given me. Now whenever I get into difficult situations and blurt out "Oh Shit" I start laughing because I know help is on the way. Feel free to make use of my angel when you are in need.

Another example of childlike behavior and humor can be found in the instructions you either read or hear from people. When it says, "sign in upon entering," write, "in upon entering." When it says, "print your name," print "your name." When the sign says "nobody allowed here," go on in and when someone shouts at you tell him or her you're a nobody. Most of the time the person will let you go, knowing that if you're that stupid you're no danger. One guard stepped in front of me and said, "I'm making you somebody, and you have to leave now."

The last point I would make is that the world is filled with pain. Why add to it? Why not help heal it? The majority of people feel the world is unfair. It isn't. It's just difficult. So make it easier for yourself and others. When people ask me "How are you feeling today?" I say "Depressed. I'm out of my anti-depressant and my doctor is away so I can't renew my prescription." Three quarters say, "I know how you feel," tell me their troubles, and offer me some of their anti-depressant, I'm not kidding. They also embrace me and help heal me, because they have been loved and have joy in their lives.

You can be a healer and spread joy through humor and laughter. The world is a human comedy if we only see it that way. Yes, it is a tragic comedy at times, but he who laughs lasts. It's not healthy to be serious and "normal." So be a carrier and spread joy and healing.

Acknowledgements

"There is no such thing as a 'self-made man.' We are made up of thousands of others. Everyone who has ever done a kind deed for us, or spoken one word of encouragement to us, has entered into the makeup of our character and of our thoughts, as well as our success."

—George Matthew Adams

If you've ever had the "pleasure" of writing a book, or know some thoroughly masochistic individual who's done it, you're aware that it's not a solo act. That's sure true of **He Who Laughs Lasts**. I've had the good fortune of getting all sorts of help and encouragement in preparing this book, and I want to take a second to say thanks to those who lent a hand.

Material, technical advice, and the encouragement I needed to help me write **He Who Laughs Lasts** came from all sorts of people, including Cheryl Heppner, Jason Slaton, Larry Littleton, Harold Horn, Jason Marshall, Judy Berman, Carolyn Ammerman, Debra

Foreman, Dick Johnson, Ernie Hairston, Karen Sadler, Neil Biddle, Bob Gsell, Ellen Safranek, Daryl and Chelsea Byrne, and Lorraine Goulet, the wonderful sister of my wife Magnificent Mary. I owe a special thanks to my friend Carolyn Piper, who not only furnished all sorts of material for the various chapters of this book, especially the one about imperfect hearing, but also provided the encouragement I needed to make this book a reality. A big hug also goes to my good friend Mark Dessert, who not only provided material for this book but proofread the manuscript before I sent it to the publisher.

Finally, I want to thank my wonderful wife Mary and fabulous family, whose love and support have helped me last. They've also reminded me of something very important—I have a brain tumor; it doesn't have me.

Introduction

Just Joking?

In April of 1987, doctors at U.C.L.A., where I was in my final trimester of studies for a Master of Fine Arts Degree in theater directing, discovered a tumor on my brainstem. So I flew to Connecticut, where I'd grown up and where my parents still lived, and had surgery at Yale-New Haven Hospital.

The operation went very well, and soon afterwards, I flew back to Los Angeles. It was a homecoming of sorts, because I'd lived in California since I graduated from Williams College in Massachusetts in the Spring of 1982. During my visit to L.A., I went to see a very special man who'd taught me in graduate school. I talked with him about all sorts of things, including the entertainment issue. His advice? Stick with the funny stuff for now. Reality, in his mind, was grim enough to make a person sick. For quite a while—years in fact—I followed his advice. It wasn't until recently that I decided to augment my entertainment options by reading and watching serious and thought-provoking books, plays, movies, and television shows.

I learned pretty soon after my first brain surgery that laughter is good for both the body and the spirit. I won't put you to sleep or keep you from the funny stuff in this book with too long an introduction, but I do want you to know some very important facts.

First, research has shown that laughter is very good for the body. It stimulates the circulation, lends a serious hand to our lungs and respiratory system, and gives us a great aerobic workout. It also lowers serum cortisol levels, increases the amount of activated T-lymphocytes in our bodies, increases the number and activity of natural killer cells, and increases the number of T-cells that have helper/receptors. To put it in English we can all understand, laughter makes us healthier. Perhaps the physiological value of laughter to the human body was best expressed by Norman Cousins, former editor of Saturday Review, who overcame a life-threatening illness with all sorts of good stuff, including plenty of humor. In **Anatomy of an Illness**, he wrote "It has always seemed to me that hearty laughter is a good way to jog internally without having to go outdoors."

Laughter is also good for the spirit. There have been all sorts of studies on the psychological benefits of laughter, but rather than trying to look halfway-intelligent by detailing them, I'll spare you and quote Mark Twain, who once said "The human race has one really effective weapon, and that is laughter. The moment it arises, all our hardnesses yield, all our irritations and resentments slip away, and a sunny spirit takes their place." I couldn't have said it better.

The bottom line? There are both physical and emotional benefits in staying "up" and finding the humor in life, no matter how hard it is at times. The average adult laughs 15 times a day, and I firmly believe that's not enough. So I hope **He Who Laughs Lasts** will help make you anything but typical.

With that in mind, I offer the following laughs and smiles, tempered by some thought-provoking facts and quotations. Much of the material in **He Who Laughs Lasts** is truly bizarre, but then again, what else would you expect from a sicko like me?

Holy Cow!

❖

How long have we humans known that humor is good for us? Well, consider this passage from one really old book—the Bible: "A merry heart doeth good like a medicine, but a broken spirit drieth the bones." *Proverbs 17:22* I guess the idea that there's a connection between mental and physical health isn't exactly new. With that in mind, I offer some religious humor that—I pray—will leave you with a merry heart.

* * * * *

Some truly hysterical (and unintentional) humor can be found in church bulletins. Bear witness to some of the strangest and funniest notices I've ever seen.

* The pastor will preach his farewell message, after which the choir will sing "Break Forth Into Joy."
* The Rev. Merriwether spoke briefly, much to the delight of the audience.
* Irving Benson and Jessie Carter were married on Oct. 24 in the church. So ends a friendship that began in school days.
* For those of you who have children and don't know it, we have a nursery downstairs.

- The choir will meet at the Larsen house for fun and sinning.
- A songfest was hell at the Methodist Church Wednesday.
- Will the ladies of the Willing Workers who have towels which belong to the kitchen please bring them to the church on Friday as we need them for supper.
- Next Sunday Mrs. Venison will be the soloist for the morning service. The pastor will then speak on "It's a Terrible Experience."
- During the absence of our pastor, we enjoyed the rare privilege of hearing a good sermon when J.F. Stubs supplied our pulpit.
- Remember in prayer the many who are sick of our church and community.
- (Reporting on an illness) GOD IS GOOD! Dr. Hargreaves is better.
- Don't let worry kill you off. Let the church help.
- Potluck supper—prayer and medication to follow.
- Smile at someone who is hard to love. Say "hell" to someone who doesn't care much about you.
- The eighth-graders will be presenting Shakespeare's **Hamlet** in the church basement on Friday at 7 p.m. The congregation is invited to this tragedy.
- Scouts are saving aluminum cans, bottles, and other items to be recycled. Proceeds will be used to cripple children.
- Ushers will eat latecomers.
- The Ladies Bible Study will be held Thursday morning at 10. All ladies are invited to lunch in the Fellowship Hall after the B.S. is done.

* The Pastor would appreciate it if the ladies of the congregation would lend him their electric girdles for the pancake breakfast next Sunday morning.
* The audience is asked to remain seated until the end of the recession.
* Low Self-Esteem Support Group will meet Thursday from 7 to 8:30 PM. Please use the back door.
* Pastor is on vacation. Massages can be given to church secretary.
* The third verse of Blessed Assurance will be sung without musical accomplishment.
* The outreach committee has enlisted 25 visitors to make calls on people who are not afflicted with any church.
* Eight new choir robes are currently needed, due to the addition of several new members and to the deterioration of some older ones.
* The choir invites any member of the congregation who enjoys sinning to join the choir.

* * * * *

Talk about llllooooonnnggggg distance! A church postcard asked recipients to check one of the following options 1) _ I have received Jesus Christ as my Lord and Savior. 2) _ I would like a personal call.

* * * * *

An old joke says that if the Three Wise Men had been Three Wise Women, they would have:
* Arrived on time

* Cleaned the stable
* Helped deliver the baby Jesus
* Made a casserole
* Brought practical gifts

I recently read another, distinctly male, take on the same question. The writer suggested that the Three Wise Women might have:
* Arrived on time, but not been sure what day it was
* Cleaned the stable, but thrown out the animals' food by mistake
* Asked for directions, but had to do it three times because they got lost twice after receiving the first two sets
* Made a casserole but burned it, so they had to order pizza
* Bought (but not brought) practical gifts, which they left in a bag at home because they were in such a hurry

* * * * *

Several years ago, a rabbi from the local temple decided to go for a quick drive around town. Unfortunately, he had an awful accident, and was rushed to the local hospital, which just happened to be run by Catholics. He was operated on, and the surgery went very well. After the operation, he was put in a room for his recovery, and became good friends with one of his nurses, who was a nun.

A few days after the move, the nurse-who-was-also-a-nun walked into the rabbi's room. She noticed that the crucifix that usually hung on the wall above the bed was missing. Perplexed, she asked him very nicely where the crucifix was. "Oh, that," said the rabbi with a sly smile "Well sister, I figured there was only enough room for one suffering Jew in here."

* * * * *

It occurs to me that the Lord, if He had been a professor, would probably never have gotten tenure. Why? Here are just a few reasons.
- He had only one major publication to his name.
- It wasn't in English.
- It was never published in a big-name journal, or submitted for peer review.
- His results probably can't be replicated.
- He doesn't want to come to class; instead, he just tells students to read the book.
- Would he expel many of his students, like he did with Adam and Eve?
- Students had to go to a mountaintop if they wanted to see Him.

And the top reason:
- Professors sometimes think of themselves as dieties, but co-workers and students just weren't comfortable with the idea of calling this one "God."

* * * * *

In case you're convinced that churches are always deeply serious places, I offer the following signs that have appeared outside various houses of God:
- Free Trip to Heaven—Details Inside!
- Try our Sundays: They are Better Than Baskin-Robbins'.
- Searching For a New Look? Have Your Faith Lifted Here!
- No God—No Peace. Know God—Know Peace.

* When down in the mouth, remember Jonah. He came out all right.
* How will you spend eternity—Smoking or Non-smoking?
* Come work for the Lord. The work is hard, the hours are long, and the pay is low. But the retirement benefits are out of this world.
* Do not wait for the hearse to take you to church
* If you're headed in the wrong direction, God allows u-turns
* This is a ch_ _ ch. What is missing? (U R)
* In the dark? Follow the Son.
* Running low on faith? Stop in for a fill-up.
* If you can't sleep, don't count sheep. Talk to the Shepherd.
* (At a church near a college) Welcome back students. God help you.

*   *   *   *   *

If the Catholic church published a dictionary, it might look like this:

AMEN: The only part of a prayer that everyone knows.

BULLETIN: 1. A newsletter filled with parish information. No one ever reads it, except during the homily. 2. A receipt that proves you attended Mass.

CHOIR: Church members whose singing gives a practical meaning to the term "hell."

HYMN: A song of praise or reflection meant to be sung three octaves higher than most humans can sing.

INCENSE: Holy Smoke!

JESUITS:	A very special group of priests famed for a particular skill—that of founding colleges with superb sports teams.
JONAH:	The original "Jaws" story.
JUSTICE:	When children grow up and have kids of their own.
KYRIE ELIEISON:	The only Greek words that most Catholics can recognize besides "gyros" and "baklava."
MAGI:	The most famous trio to attend a baby shower.
MANGER:	1. Where Mary had to give birth to Jesus because Joseph didn't have health insurance. 2. The Good Book's reminder that holiday travel has always been rough.
PEW:	A medieval torture device still found in Catholic churches.
PROCESSION:	A ceremonial formation at the beginning of Mass, which consists of altar boys and girls, the celebrant, and late parishioners desperately hunting for seats.
RECESSION:	The ceremonial procession at the conclusion of Mass—led by parishioners trying to beat the crowd to the parking lot.
RELICS:	People who have attended Mass for so many years they actually know when to sit, kneel, and stand.
USHERS:	Members of the parish who have serious counting problems, particularly when it comes to knowing the seating capacity of a pew.

* * * * *

Children have their own—and very special—"take" on religious history. Here are just a few holy "facts" offered by young people.

* In the first book of the Bible, Guinessis, God got tired of creating the world, so he took the Sabbath off.
* Adam and Eve were created from an apple tree.
* Moses led the Hebrews to the Red Sea, where they made unleavened bread, which is bread without any ingredients.
* The Egyptians were all drowned in the dessert.
* Noah built an ark, which the animals came onto in pears.
* Lot's wife was a pillar of salt by day, but a ball of fire by night.
* Moses died before he ever reached Canada.
* Joshua led the Hebrews in the battle of Geritol.
* The greatest miracle in the Bible is when Joshua told his son to stand still and he obeyed him.
* David was a Hebrew king skilled at playing the liar. He fought with the Finklesteins, a race of people who lived in Biblical times.
* Solomon, one of David's sons, had 300 wives and 700 porcupines.
* When Mary heard that she was the mother of Jesus, she sang the Magna Carta.
* Martin Luther was on a diet of worms.
* The first commandment was when Eve told Adam to eat the apple.
* The fifth commandment is to humor thy father and mother.
* The seventh commandment is thou shalt not admit adultery.
* Jesus enunciated the Golden Rule, which says to do one to others before they do one to you.

* St. Paul cavorted to Christianity. He preached holy acrimony, which is another name for marriage.
* A Christian should have only one spouse. This is called monotony.

* * * * *

Not long ago, a little boy went up to his Pastor after a service and said "When I grow up, I'm going to give you some money."

The Pastor was delighted and replied, "How wonderful!" He was also curious, and asked "But why?"

The boy's reply? "Well, my daddy says you're the poorest preacher we've ever had."

* * * * *

Then there was the five-year-old who prayed, "And forgive us our trash baskets as we forgive those who put trash in our baskets."

* * * * *

A six-year-old girl and her four-year-old brother went to church with their parents one day. The boy giggled and talked out loud over and over. After putting up with the noise for a long time, the sister leaned over and told the boy."You're supposed to keep it quiet in church. No talking and no giggling" The boy was saddened to hear this, but he wasn't about to give up. "Who's going to stop me?" he asked. The sister's response? "The hushers."

* * * * *

Jesus and Satan were in the midst of a heavy argument as to who was more of a computer whiz. They couldn't stop fighting, and God, who was listening, was getting tired all of the bickering. So He told them, "Compute away for three hours! I'll read everything you create and decide who's better."

Satan and Jesus agreed, sat down at their respective computer keyboards, and worked ferociously for three hours. They moused, did spread-sheets, wrote reports, and sent faxes and e-mails. They downloaded, researched and wrote genealogy reports, and made cards. If it could be done on a computer, they did it.

The test was only ten minutes from completion when lightning flashed, thunder rolled, rain poured, and the electricity went off. Jesus sighed, and Satan, staring at his blank computer screen, shouted every curse word you can imagine.

After a few minutes, the electricity came back on. Jesus and Satan both re-booted their computers. But Satan couldn't find any of the work he'd done. It had all disappeared when the electricity went out. "It's gone! It's all gone!," Satan screamed. "I lost everything when the power went out!"

Jesus, though, found all the work He'd done, and started printing it out. Satan was—to say the least—really upset that the power outage had been a disaster for him and hadn't seriously affected Jesus. "How did he do that?" Satan asked God. The Lord shrugged and said, "Jesus saves."

*   *   *   *   *

One sunny day not too long ago a Catholic priest, a Lutheran minister, and a Baptist pastor went out fishing on a lake together. The three of them were sitting in a rowboat in the middle of the lake, and the priest announced he was going to shore to get a soda. He stepped very gracefully out of the boat, and walked to the shore—on the water! He got his soda, and walked back to the boat the same way. After the priest came back to the boat, the Lutheran minister decided he wanted a soda as well, and did exactly what the priest had done.

The Baptist pastor, not wanting to appear any less holy than the priest or the minister, said to the two of them, "My faith is as strong as yours, and I can walk on water too." So the pastor stepped out of the boat. But he sank right away. The Priest turned to the minister and asked: "Think we should tell him where the sandbar is?"

✶   ✶   ✶   ✶   ✶

Her young students were getting ready to head to a church service after Sunday School, and the teacher asked the children why it was necessary to be quiet in church.One student replied "Because people are sleeping."

✶   ✶   ✶   ✶   ✶

A preacher was concerned that his congregation couldn't hear his homilies, so he decided to use a lapel microphone. He was delighted with the freedom and confidence the mike gave him, and the Sunday after he'd been hooked up, he moved briskly around the platform, accompanied by his new microphone and its cord.

The cord gave him some trouble, though, and he got wound up in it and nearly tripped several times. A little girl who was sitting in a pew near the altar saw the minister fight with the cord repeatedly. She leaned over and asked her mother "If he gets loose, will he hurt us?"

✶   ✶   ✶   ✶   ✶

A mother was teaching her three-year-old daughter the Lord's Prayer. After several evenings of repeating it after her mother, the daughter decided she wanted to fly solo. The mother listened with pride as the daughter got it totally right—until she got to the end, that is, when she said: "Lead us not into temp-tation, but deliver us some e-mail. Amen."

*   *   *   *   *

A small boy was asked to serve in his cousin's wedding. He readily agreed. In the procession, he repeatedly took two steps, stopped, and turned to the crowd. He would then put his hands up (sort of like claws) and roar …. step, step, ROAR, step, step, ROAR…. The crowd was delighted, and laughed bigtime. The little boy wasn't delighted by all the laughter, though. He was mystified. As he said later: "I was just being the Ring Bear."

*   *   *   *   *

Speaking of bears, here's a true story:
There was a little boy who was upset because his family decided not to go to church one Sunday. He cried and carried on. His mom asked the boy why he was so upset. He said he wanted to visit the cross-eyed bear. The mother was totally baffled.
The following Sunday at church while the choir was singing, the boy said, "See, Mommy. They are singing about the crossed eyed bear." She laughed because the choir was singing "The Cross I'd Bear."

*   *   *   *   *

Two doctors and an HMO manager died and lined up for admission to heaven. St. Peter asked each one to say why he should be admitted.

The first doctor stepped forward and said; "I was a pediatrician and worked at a free clinic for parents and their children."

"Wonderful," said St. Peter. "You can enter."

The second doctor then stepped forward and said; "I was a psychiatrist for my town. I helped folks solve their emotional problems."

"You, too, may enter" said St. Peter.

The HMO manager stepped forward and said; "I was a HMO manager. I helped people get cost-effective health care."

After a slight pause, St. Peter said; "You may come in as well."

As the HMO manager walked by, however, St. Peter added, "You can only stay three days, though. After that you can go to hell."

School Daze

Back in the Dark Ages (well, about ten years ago, actually), I was a college professor. I had to call it quits, though, when my hearing decided to take a permanent Spring Break (it's kind of hard to teach hearing students when your ears don't work!). I still have a special love for humor that comes from the academic world, though, and probably always will. So here are some educational eye-openers. Most of them are true too. I hope this chapter gets an "A" from you.

*   *   *   *   *

Need to brush up on your history? These historical "facts" provided by students at various schools might help.

* Pompeii was destroyed by an overflow of saliva from the Vatican.
* In 328 B.C. Rome was invaded by the Gals.
* Julius Caesar was renowned for his great strength. He threw a bridge across the Rhine. His dying words were "And you too—you brute."
* Rome was invaded by the ballbearings.
* Martin Luther was on a diet of worms.

* The death of Queen Elizabeth I ended an error.
* John Paul Jones became one of America's greatest nasal heroes.
* In the middle of the 18th century all the morons moved to Utah.
* The capital of Ethiopia is Adidas Ababa.
* The process of putting a president on trial is known as impalement.
* During the first twenty years of the century, there was much suffrage from women.
* The leader of the Bolsheviks was John Lennon.
* They are fighting a civil war in Serbia because the Bostonians, Crates, and Hertzgodivas want to get rid of the Serves.
* During his term of office, Woodrow Wilson had many foreign affairs.
* The inhabitants of Egypt were called mummies. They lived in the Sarah Dessert and traveled by Camelot.
* In the Olympic Games, Greeks ran races, jumped, hurled the biscuits, and threw the java.
* History calls people Romans because they never stayed in one place for very long. At Roman banquets, the guests wore garlic in their hair.
* Nero was a cruel tyrant who would torture his poor subjects by playing the fiddle to them.
* Madman Curie discovered radium.
* Karl Marx became one of the Marx Brothers.
* Queen Victoria was the longest queen. She sat on a thorn for 63 years.

* Bach was the most famous composer in the world, and so was Handel. Handel was half German, half Italian, and half English. He was very large. Bach died from 1750 to the present.
* Delegates from the original thirteen states formed the Contented Congress.

*   *   *   *   *

Kids who miss school usually need to bring in an excuse note signed by a parent or guardian. Here are a few of the funniest ones I've ever seen.

* Please excuse Mary for being absent. She was sick and I had her shot.
* Please ecksuse John from being absent on Jan. 28, 29, 30, 31,32, and also 33.
* Please excuse Roland from P.E. for a few days. Yesterday he fell out of a tree and misplaced his hip.
* John has been absent because he had two teeth taken off his face.
* Mary could not come to school because she has been bothered by very close veins.
* Chris will not be in school cus he has an acre in his side.
* Please excuse Harriet for missing school yesterday. We forgot to get the Sunday paper off the porch, and when we found it Monday, we thought it was Sunday.
* Please excuse my son's tardiness. I forgot to wake him up, and I did not find him until I started making the beds.
* My son is under the doctor's care and should not take P. E. today. Please execute him.
* Please excuse Raul from school yesterday. He had a stomach egg.

- * Stanley had to miss some school. He had an attack of whooping cranes in his chest.
- * Ralph was absent yesterday because of a sore trout.
- * I kept Monica at home today because she was not feeling too bright.
- * The basement of our house got flooded where the children sleep, so they had to be evaporated.

*   *   *   *   *

Well, it's a start … A fourth-grade teacher gave her students a list of beginnings of famous sayings, and asked them to finish them. Here are just a few of the conclusions they provided:

- * The grass is always greener… …when you leave the sprinkler on!
- * A rolling stone… …plays the guitar!
- * A bird in the hand is… …a real mess.
- * No news is… …no newspaper.
- * It's always darkest… …just before I open my eyes.
- * We have nothing to fear but… …homework.
- * If you can't stand the heat… …go swimming.
- * Never put off 'til tomorrow what… …you should have done yesterday.
- * A penny saved is … …nothing in the real world.
- * To err is human… …To eat a muskrat is not.
- * I think, therefore… …I get a headache.
- * Better to light a candle than… …to light an explosive.

* A journey of a thousand miles begins with…   …a blister.
* There is nothing new under…   …the bed.
* Laugh and the world laughs with you. Cry and…   …someone yells "Shut up!"
* Don't count your chickens…   …it takes too long.

* * * * *

You probably remember those days when you were a college student. In case your memory is a little hazy, though, here are a few reminders of what it means.

*   You average three hours of sleep per night.
*   You get more sleep in class than in your room.
*   You wake up four minutes before class.
*   You need a shovel to find the floor of your dorm room.
*   Your regular breakfast is a soda swilled on the way to class.
*   You personally keep the local pizza joint in the black.
*   You wear the same pair of blue jeans every day for three weeks without doing your laundry.
*   Your main source of exercise is running to class.
*   You regularly write checks for "princely" sums like 46 cents.
*   Your major source of social activity is a trip to the library.
*   You decide you want to feed the poor, so you buy yourself some Ramen noodles.

* * * * *

On the other hand, you probably work in education if:
* You can speak fluent schoolese.
* You give your spouse "that look" for misbehaving.
* You refer to adult friends as "boys and girls."
* You decide not to have children of your own because you can't think of names for them that wouldn't seriously raise your blood pressure.
* You think all people should be required to have a government permit in order to reproduce, and it can only be granted after they work in a school for at least five years.
* You believe that caffeine should be available in pill and IV form.
* You meet a student's parents and immediately say to yourself "Now I understand why that kid is like that."

AND MOST TELLING SIGN:

* You want to choke the next person who says something like "it must be great to work only eight to three and have your summers free."

*   *   *   *   *

Remember those tests we used to have to take when we were in school? Well, here are some actual excerpts from science exam papers:
* Three kinds of blood vessels are arteries, vanes, and caterpillars.
* The dodo is a bird that is almost decent by now.
* The process of turning steam back into water again is called conversation.
* The Earth makes one resolution every 24 hours.

* The pistol of a flower is its only protection against insects.
* If conditions are not favorable, bacteria go into a period of adolescence.
* Dew is formed on leaves when the sun shines down on them and makes them perspire.
* A triangle which has an angle of 135 degrees is called an obscene triangle.
* A person should take a bath once in the summer, and not quite so often in the winter.
* When you haven't got enough iodine in your blood you get a glacier.
* Humans are more intelligent than beasts because human branes have more convulsions.
* For head colds: use an agonizer to spray the nose until it drops in your throat.
* Before giving a blood transfusion, find out if the blood is affirmative or negative.
* When water freezes you can walk on it. That is what Christ did long ago in wintertime.
* When you smell an odorless gas, it is probably carbon monoxide.

* * * * *

Speaking of tests, there's been a lot of talk lately about the easy admission standards colleges have for scholarship athletes. Here's a sample test they must take.

To be completed in: One Month
1. What is the principal language of English people?
2. Discuss in detail the Marxian approach to economic and social conditions, OR give the first name of Margaret Thatcher.
3. Playwright and poet William Shakespeare was well-known for:
   (a) writing
   (b) architecture
   (c) commerce
   (b) navigation
4. The Pope, who heads the Catholic church, is:
   (a) Catholic
   (b) Jewish
   (c) Hindu
   (d) Agnostic
5. Many countries use the metric system of measurement. How many feet are there in 0.0 meters?
6. What time is it when the big hand is on the 12 and the little hand is on the 5?
7. Moses received the ten commandments from the Lord. How many were there?
8. What are people who live in America's north called?
   (a) Westerners
   (b) Southerners
   (c) Northerners
9. Spell the last names of U.S. presidents Bill Clinton, George Bush, and Ronald Reagan.

_____
_____
_____

10. Where does rain come from?
    (a) Wal-Mart
    (b) The Weather Channel
    (c) China
    (d) The sky

      *   *   *   *   *

Feeling old? This true story is definitely for you then. A college history professor was asked to teach a course in medieval history. He agreed, and on the first day of class he asked the students why they were taking the course. "Because" replied one freshman, "I really like the 1800's."

      *   *   *   *   *

Your college grades go a long way to determining the rest of your life. Did you know that each department has its own approach to determining a student's grades?

* DEPARTMENT OF STATISTICS:

    —Grades are plotted along the bell curve.

* DEPARTMENT OF PSYCHOLOGY:

    —All students are tested using ink blots. They should blot ink in their exam books, close them, and turn them in. The professor, when feeling suitably validated, will open the books and assign whatever grade comes to mind.

- DEPARTMENT OF HISTORY:
  —Students will be given whatever grade they got last year.
- DEPARTMENT OF RELIGION:
  —All grades are determined by God.
- DEPARTMENT OF PHILOSOPHY:
  —What does a grade really mean?
- DEPARTMENT OF MATHEMATICS:
  —All grades are variable.
- DEPARTMENT OF COMPUTER SCIENCE:
  —All grades are determined by random-number-generator software.
- DEPARTMENT OF MUSIC :
  —The department's students will learn their grade by listening to the instructor play the corresponding note. Sharps and flats will be used to indicate pluses and minuses.
- DEPARTMENT OF FINANCE:
  —All students must invest in the stock market. Grades will be determined by the return on their investments.
- DEPARTMENT OF ACCOUNTING:
  —Any student who survives an IRS audit will be given an "A."

* * * * *

A mother was doing some housework in the kitchen one weekday morning, and decided to go wake up her son. "Time to go to school," she said to him.

"Mother," the son replied: "I don't want to go. No one in the school likes me."

"The kids hate me, the teachers don't like me, the superintendent is trying to transfer me, and the school board wants me to quit. Even the school bus drivers think I'm a jerk."

"Son," the mother replied, "you have to go to school. You're healthy, and you have plenty to learn and teach others." "Besides," she added, "you're 47 years old and you're the principal."

* * * * *

A true story: On the first day of the Spring semester recently, a college teacher went to the cafeteria, and saw three students hard at work on their calculators. The professor was amazed they'd received such a tough problem so early in the semester, and asked them what they were working on. One replied "We're figuring out how many days there are until Spring Break."

* * * * *

A little girl came home after her first day of school "What did you learn today?" her mother asked. "Not much," the girl replied. "I have to go back tomorrow."

* * * * *

A foreigner who was touring the United States found himself on a college campus. He stopped a lad who was passing him and asked the name of the school. The reply? "Sorry sir, I don't know. I'm just a football player here."

* * * * *

Let's finish this chapter with a true story. An eighth grade class was discussing how to raise funds, and one of the students said "Let's have a topless carwash." The teacher had never heard the term before, and was totally confused. So she asked what the student meant. "Well, we can't reach them" said the student, "so we won't wash the tops of the cars."

Oh, You Animal!

◆

I confess it—I'm a serious animal-lover. Since we became a team back in 1988, my wife and I have had a rabbit, three cats, a pair of birds, and all sorts of goldfish. And I've loved them all! I've also learned that animals can be a major source of laughter. Here are some of my favorite creature-related jokes. I hope you'll enjoy them, you animal!

* * * * *

Ever wondered about that age-old question "Why did the chicken cross the road?" I got to thinking about how a few people would have answered it, and offer some possibilities.

* SIGMUND FREUD: Mother love.
* PLATO: For the greater good.
* JERRY FALWELL: Obviously, the chicken was gay. It crossed the road because it wanted to go to the "other side" and have "a good time." If you want to become gay too, just eat chicken! I recommend we all boycott eating chicken until we eliminate the liberal abomination of homosexuality.

- PAT BUCHANAN: That commie chicken obviously wanted to steal a job from a hard-working American.
- SHAKESPEARE: Isn't this much ado about nothing?
- KARL MARX : Class consciousness.
- MAE WEST: Because I invited it to come up and see me some time.
- MARK TWAIN: The news of the crossing has been greatly exaggerated.
- CAPTAIN JAMES T. KIRK: To boldly go where no chicken has gone before.
- OLIVER NORTH: It was a matter of National Security.
- ERNEST HEMINGWAY: To die. In the rain.
- ROBERT FROST: To cross the road less traveled.
- MARTIN LUTHER KING, JR: I dream of a world where all chickens can cross whatever road they please.
- KEN STARR: My investigation will prove that the chicken crossed the road on orders from the president of the United States of America. The chicken is clearly no more than a pawn in the president's ongoing attempt to disregard the law.
- ALBERT EINSTEIN: Did the chicken really cross the road? Perhaps the road moved beneath the chicken. It's all relative, you know.
- TIMOTHY LEARY: Because the Establishment wouldn't have allowed it to take any other kind of trip.
- COLONEL SANDERS: Oh darn—I must have missed one!

* * * * *

Speaking of chickens, have you ever wondered why chicken coops have two doors? Well, if they had four doors they'd be chicken sedans.

* * * * *

Cats are generally very clean pets, but there are times when you'll have to give yours a bath . Here's a procedure you might want to try.

1. Start by thoroughly cleaning the toilet.
2. Add the appropriate amount of shampoo to the toilet water.
3. Lovingly hold the cat close to you, and comfort him while you carry him towards the bathroom.
4. With all the gentleness you can muster, place the cat in the toilet.
5. Close the lid and pray extensively (You might want to stand on the lid so the cat won't escape)
6. Flush the toilet repeatedly (three or four times should do it). This will "power-wash and rinse" the cat.
7. Ask your spouse to open the door to the outside. Be sure no humans are standing between the toilet and that door.
8. Stand behind the toilet (I recommend you stand as far behind it as you can). Quickly lift the lid.
9. The cat will exit the toilet extremely quickly, then sprint out of the bathroom and scamper outside, where it will dry itself.
10. Say a prayer of gratitude expressing your thanks that you don't need to bathe your cat too often. Then read (or re-read) **Grime and Punishment.**

* * * * *

Why should you opt for a pet instead of children? Here are just eight reasons.

* Veterinarians have evening hours. Pediatricians don't.
* If you decide to take your pet to the movies, it won't disturb the other moviegoers with its crying. If you choose not to take it with you, though, you won't have to struggle with finding a sitter.
* Pets don't grow out of adorable (and expensive!) clothes in three months.
* Kittens still look cute if they haven't had a bath in a month.
* Pets don't go to college, so you won't have to lie awake nights thinking about how you can possibly pay for your pet's higher education.
* You can pet an animal without being accused of sexual harrasment.
* Women don't have to worry about being charged with destroying the moral fabric of the country if they aren't married to the father of their pets.
* You don't have to worry about being questioned about your ability to do your job well when your boss hears that you just got a pet.

* * * * *

In December of 1996 the *Arizona Republic* reported on animal psychologist Krista Cantrell, who credits her success with dogs to the fact that she can communicate telepathically with them. As a result, she can understand most master-dog relationship problems. She's developed a big following too—several dog owners who've employed Cantrell speak very highly of her. Cantrell's special skill isn't limited to understanding dogs either. A horse who was about to be put to sleep told Cantrell that he was simply over-medicated. Cantrell told the owner, and just over a month later, the horse won a race.

* * * * *

Did you hear about the boy who received a parrot for his birthday? This wasn't a baby parrot either : it was fully grown. It also had what can only be called "a bad attitude.' It spoke well, but its vocabulary was really offensive: it swore all the time.

The boy loved the bird, though, and worked hard to change its attitude. He constantly spoke gently with the bird, and played soft music for it. He tried everything to soften the bird's heart. But nothing worked. One day the parrot started his usual rudeness routine, and the boy got so angry that he put the parrot in the freezer.

At first, the bird squawked and screamed. But then suddenly, there was total silence. The boy was terrified—he was afraid that the parrot had died. So he opened the freezer door. The parrot stepped calmly from the freezer and very solemnly apologized for swearing at the boy. The parrot didn't stop there, though. "May I ask," he said, "what the chicken did?"

* * * * *

Ever wonder about what a dog really thinks? Well, these guidelines from a dog's handbook might give you a hint.
- * VISITORS: Some people are actually afraid of dogs. To find out if a visitor belongs to that club, race across the room as you bark loudly. Leap playfully on the visitor. Growl ferociously and lick the human's face. If s/he falls on the floor and starts crying, it's pretty likely you're not looking at a dog-lover.

* BARKING: As a dog, you'll be expected to bark regularly. So bark—a LOT. When you're hungry or in need of some petting, it's important to let out a bark. Your owners will think you're protecting their house. That's especially true late at night when they're sleeping soundly in their beds. Humans actually like to wake up in the middle of the night as long as they think you're barking for the 'right" reason.
* LICKING: There is a fine art to licking. Learn how to do it well, For starters: always take a BIG drink from your water dish before you lick a human.
* SNIFFING: Humans love to be sniffed. Everywhere. As the family dog, you must accommodate them.
* DOORS: You must always sleep in the area directly in front of a door.
* DINING ETIQUETTE: You must always sit under the table at dinner. This is especially true when your owner has guests. You should clean up any food that falls on the floor (it's a dirty job, but someone has to do it!).
* HOUSEBREAKING: Humans are very concerned about housebreaking. Therefore, you should break as much of the house as possible.
* COUCHES: You are encouraged to lie on all couches. A new one, however, should be laid on only after all humans in the house have gone to bed.
* CHASING CATS: When chasing cats, remember the saying "Process, not product." Never quite catch cats. The fun is in the chase.

* CHEWING: Support the fashion industry. Eat a shoe.
* HOLES: Digging holes can be a tricky business. I encourage you to dig a bunch of small ones rather than one large one. If you do that, your humans might think it's the work of gophers instead of you. There are never enough holes in the ground, and I encourage you to help end this tragedy.

* * * * *

You might ask why dogs don't use computers. Well, there are lots of reasons. Here are just a few:

* They can't stick their heads out the latest version of Windows.
* The "fetch" command isn't available on all platforms.
* Ever try to read a monitor with your head cocked to one side?
* "Marking" every web site they visit would take hours!
* Dogs have a burning need to attack the screen whenever they hear "You've Got Mail."
* It's really hard for them to hide the fact that they're browsing www.pethouse.com when their tails keep wagging.
* The Chuckwagon Screen Saver is sooooo hard to find.
* There's still no emoticon that signifies tail-wagging.
* They're afraid of developing Carpal Paw Syndrome.
* Barking in the next cubicle would activate their voice recognition software.
* SniffU/SniffMe is still in the beta-test stage.
* Learning SIT and STAY was tough enough. They definitely don't want to master GREP and AWK.

- Maneuvering a saliva-coated mouse would be really tough.
- There are no newsgroups with pictures of a master's leg.

THE TOP REASON:
- One definition of dog hell is: "Typing with paws."

* * * * *

Cats, however, are big fans of computers. You can tell if your feline is using yours if:
- You start getting a lot of e-mail from someone named "Fluffy."
- There are traces of kitty litter on your keyboard.
- You find yourself subscribed to a list called "alt.recreational.catnip."
- Your mouse has teeth marks in it.
- You discover that hate-mail to Microsoft about their release of "CyberDog" has been sent from your computer.
- New software like "WarCat II" starts showing up around your house.

THE BIGGEST HINT:
- In on-line chat your screen-name is "IronMouser."

* * * * *

Ever notice these things about cats?
- They do whatever they want whenever they feel like it.
- They almost never listen to you.

* They're totally unpredictable.
* They whine when they're unhappy.
* They expect you to cater to their every whim.
* They're moody.
* They leave hair everywhere.
* They drive you nuts.
* They cost an arm and a leg.

How about dogs?

* They lie around all day, and only on the most comfortable furniture in the house.
* They can hear a package of food opening half a block away but can't hear you when you're in the same room.
* They can look dumb and lovable at the same time.
* They growl when they're unhappy.
* They are great at begging.
* They will love you forever if you rub their tummies.
* They leave their toys everywhere.

Obviously, cats are little women in fur coats and dogs are very short, furry men.

*   *   *   *   *

My friend Jason woke up one morning to find his dog wasn't moving at all. Jason was—to put it mildly—deeply concerned. He called a vet and told her the dog wasn't moving, and the vet told Jason to bring his dog in as soon as possible.

Jason and the dog arrived at the vet's office a few minutes later. The vet took a look at the dog and said "Your dog is dead." Jason was aghast, and asked the vet if there was anything else she could do. The vet didn't know if anything else could be done, but offered to try one more thing. Jason said "please try it, whatever it is."

So the vet left the room and returned in less than a minute carrying a large cage with a cat in it. The vet opened the cage door and the cat walked over to the dog. The cat sniffed the dog from head to toe, and walked all over it. Nothing happened. The cat walked back to the cage.

"That proves it." the vet said to Jason. "Your dog is dead."

Jason was crushed, but appreciative of the vet's efforts. "How much do I owe you?" he asked. "That will be $300." the vet replied. Jason was aghast. "Why so much?" he asked. "Well," came the reply, "it's $25 for the office visit and $275 for the cat scan."

*   *   *   *   *

Some important (?) animal trivia you might want to know:
- *   TTHHFFPPTT!! A crocodile can't stick its tongue out.
- *   I thought I slept a lot, but I've learned that a snail can sleep for three years straight.
- *   Polar bears must be leftists, because every one of them is left-handed. Bats must be liberals too: they always turn left when exiting a cave. Ants are probably conservatives, though, because an intoxicated one always falls over to its right.
- *   My wife and I are both serious cat lovers, so I'm happy to report that cats (even if I can't hear them) can make over one hundred vocal sounds. Dogs, by contrast, can make about ten.
- *   Finland banned Donald Duck comics because he doesn't wear pants.
- *   Don't try to teach your elephant to jump for joy: elephants are the only animals that can't jump.

* I wouldn't say that starfish aren't too bright, but they don't have a brain.
* The good taste award goes to catfish, who have over 27,000 taste buds.
* Do you really need yours? Some insects can live up to a year without their heads.
* The flying gurnard, a fish, swims in water, walks on land, and flies through the air.
* Be careful about raising a stink around certain animals. Elephants can smell water three miles away, and male emperor moths can smell female ones up to seven miles away.
* You can buy a toupee for your dog in Tokyo.

Food Fight!

♦

People are really concerned about what and how well they eat. With good reason too: food is an important part of our health. It's also a major source of funny stuff. Here's a serving that provides much more than the minimum daily adult requirement of laughter and smiles.

* * * * *

Let's start by looking at some kitchen-isms. The following sayings were posted in various kitchens.

- * A Messy Kitchen is a Happy Kitchen, and This Kitchen is Delirious
- * No Husband Has Ever Been Shot While Doing the Dishes
- * A Balanced Diet is a Cookie in Each Hand
- * Thou Shalt Not Weigh More Than Thy Refrigerator
- * A Clean House is a Sign of a Misspent Life
- * Help Keep the Kitchen Clean—Eat Out
- * Countless Numbers of People Have Eaten in This Kitchen and Gone On to Lead Normal Lives
- * My Next House Will Have No Kitchen—Just Vending Machines

* * * * *

The translation of certain food and drink slogans from English to a foreign language has led to some real hilarity.

* The Spanish translation of the phrase "Got Milk?" meant "Are you lactating?"
* The translation of Pepsi's "Come Alive with the Pepsi Generation" into Chinese communicated a thoroughly scary message: "Pepsi Brings Your Ancestors Back from the Grave."
* The slogan "It takes a strong man to make a tender chicken," which many Perdue customers know, didn't translate into Spanish very well: the translation meant "it takes an aroused man to make a chicken affectionate."
* A Coca-Cola slogan when translated into Chinese meant "Bite the wax tadpole" or "female horse stuffed with wax," depending on what dialect was used.

* * * * *

You might have heard the term "real food." Well, here's a "real story" about grub. A woman went to her regular diner, and ordered breakfast. But it arrived with three sausages instead of the usual four. The woman asked what was up, and the waitress explained that the cook had accidentally dropped one of the customer's sausages. The fourth, the waitress promised, would be ready soon. Moments later, the cook dashed out of the kitchen with the new sausage on a platter, and said to the customer "Here you are. The missing link."

* * * * *

The Patriot-News of Harrisburg, Pennsylvania ran a picture of an overturned truck that carried 43,000 pounds of cheesecake and had delayed traffic for hours when it fell over. The headline of the accompanying story? "Cheesecake Clogs Artery."

* * * * *

Looking for a diet? There are lots of good ones, but here are five you might want to avoid.
* The Will Rogers Diet: "I never met a food I didn't like."
* The Accountant's Diet: You don't eat—you just count your beans.
* The Adam Diet: An apple pie a day keeps the doctor away.
* The Baseball Diet: Three steaks and you're out.
* The Seafood Diet : When you see food, you eat it.

* * * * *

Speaking of diets: if you believe in saving the best for last, here's a diet that you should be able to relate to:

BREAKFAST

1/2 grapefruit
1 slice whole wheat toast
8 ounces skim milk

* * * * *

LUNCH

4 oz. tofu
1 cup steamed carrots
1 cup herbal tea—no milk, no sugar

*   *   *   *   *

MID-AFTERNOON SNACK

1 medium apple

*   *   *   *   *

DINNER

1 loaf garlic bread (Parmesan cheese essential)
1 large pizza (with mozzarella cheese and your choice of meat)
Four cans non-diet soda or one pitcher of beer
Three candy bars of your choice

*   *   *   *   *

Approved evening snacks:

* One package peanut butter cookies.
* Half gallon of mint-chocolate chip ice cream with one jar of hot fudge sauce. Nuts, cherries, and whipped cream should be added as needed.
* Cheesecake (whole only)

* Ice cream (half-gallon or more)
* Chocolate (any type and in hhhhuuuggggeeee amounts)

There are a few things you should know before you embark on this diet.

* As long as no one sees you eat something, it has no calories.
* Whenever you eat a candy bar, drink a diet soda. The calories in the candy bar will be canceled out by the soda.
* When you eat with others, be sure to eat less than they do. Calories don't count if you do that.
* Break up cookies before you eat them. Why? Because cookie pieces contain no calories. Breaking up cookies causes calorie leakage.
* Foods of the same color have the same number of calories. For example, broccoli and mint chocolate ice cream are equal in calories.
* Food licked off knives and spoons when preparing something has no calories. Examples: Peanut butter on a knife when you're making a sandwich; ice cream on a spoon while making a sundae.
* Eat while standing up. Food eaten when you're upright has no calories. Researchers aren't sure why this is true, but suspect it has to do with gravity. Apparently, calories bypass the body of the vertical eater, flowing down the legs, through the soles of the feet, and into the floor. Walking while you eat is also helpful. For instance, ice cream bars or hot dogs eaten at a fair or amusement park actually have negative calorie counts.
* Food eaten in front of televisions is calorie-free. TVs emit small amounts of radiation, which eliminates both the calories in the food eaten in front of them and all recollections of having eaten at all.

* The person putting pies and cakes away should straighten up the edge. This can be achieved by slicing off and eating any offending irregularities. These have no calories.
* Calories in food eaten for medicinal purposes don't count. This includes hot chocolate, malted milk, toast, cheesecake, and all other foods consumed for psychological health.
* Foods such as ice cream, sour cream, and butter act as poultices and draw out the calories of any food they're placed upon, leaving them calorie-free.
* Food on toothpicks is calorie-free. Cheese and crackers, sausages, and mini-franks are generally considered fattening, but if you stick them on toothpicks, the calories in them leak out the bottom.
* Food bought for charitable reasons, such as Girl Scout cookies, bake-sale cakes, food eaten at ice cream socials, and yummies purchased at church strawberry festivals all have religious dispensation from calories.

*   *   *   *   *

A true story: a woman was at her doctor's office, and saw a clerk licking and sealing a bunch of envelopes. Two office employees had tried to convince the clerk to use a sponge instead of her tongue for wetting the envelopes, because of the risk of paper cuts from the envelope and illness from the glue. Neither had any impact, though. But when the departing patient told the clerk that there's one-tenth of a calorie in the glue on a standard envelope, the clerk started running around frantically, looking for a sponge.

*   *   *   *   *

Want to burn some calories without working out? Try these activities.

Activity	Calories burned
Beating around the bush	85
Jumping to conclusions	125
Swallowing your pride	250
Passing the buck	300
Pushing your luck	200
Making mountains out of molehills	450
Wading through paperwork	275
Bending over backwards	175
Jumping on the bandwagon	150
Running around in circles	250
Eating crow	225
Climbing the ladder of success	725
Adding fuel to the fire	175
Putting your foot in your mouth	325
Banging your head against the wall	150

∗ ∗ ∗ ∗ ∗

My friend Paul is—to put it politely—a big eater. Actually, he's about the size of a small house. But that's another story. I saw him recently, and he looked very depressed. So I asked him what was wrong. With tears in his eyes, he replied,

"The all-you-can-eat restaurants in town have banned me."

∗ ∗ ∗ ∗ ∗

My best friend is seriously addicted to chocolate. Heck, the tag-line she uses on her e-mails is:"Chocolate—it's not just for breakfast anymore." So I've done a little research on the subject. Here are a few things you might want to know:

* Chocolate-covered strawberries, raisins, and cherries count as fruit, so you can eat as many as you want.
* Chocolate should be stored on top of your refrigerator. Chocolate calories are afraid of heights and will jump out of the chocolate in an effort to protect themselves.
* Chocolate performs an important economic role. Without it, there might be no demand for one-size-fits-all clothing.
* If you're concerned about eating right, you should know that eating both dark and white chocolate provides you with a balanced meal.
* There is no organization like Chocaholics Anonymous because no one wants to quit eating the sweet stuff.

     ✷   ✷   ✷   ✷   ✷

A man who was a rather big drinker and not exactly a connoisseur of fine wine stumbled into a bar and yelled to the bartender "Gimme a bottle of wine!" "Of course sir," the bartender replied, "what year?" The man's response? "What year? I want it right now!"

     ✷   ✷   ✷   ✷   ✷

Here's a true story that might make you sick.

A man who was staying at a seaside hotel went to the inn's restaurant for breakfast for the second day in a row. He called over the headwaiter and said, "I'd like two boiled eggs, one of them so undercooked that it's runny, and the other so over-cooked that it's tough and hard to eat. I also want grilled bacon that has been left on the plate to get cold; burnt toast that crumbles away as soon as I touch it with a knife, frozen butter that's impossible to spread, and a pot of very weak, lukewarm coffee."

"That's a very complicated order sir," the baffled waiter said. "It might be quite difficult to fill."

"Oh really?" the guest replied, "That's what I got yesterday!"

* * * * *

A mother took her 5-year-old son Johnny with her to the bank on a busy Friday. They were in line behind a rather obese lady wearing a business suit, As the mother patiently waited, Johnny looked at the women in front of him and observed loudly, "Hey, Mom, she's REALLY FAT."

The woman looked at Johnny, made eye contact with his mother, and gave her an understanding smile. Johnny received a quiet reprimand from his mom.

After a minute or two, Johnny spread his hands as far as they would go and loudly said, "I bet her butt is **that** wide."

At this, the overweight lady glared at Johnny. His embarrassed mother severely scolded her son.

After a couple of minutes Johnny stated loudly, "Look how the fat hangs over her belt."

The overweight lady turned and told Johnny's mother to control her rude child. Johnny's mother threatened him with his very life and existence.

Things in the bank were quiet. The obese lady had moved to the front of the line when her pager began to emit its distinctive beeps.

Johnny was panicked and said at the top of his voice, "RUN FOR YOUR LIFE MOM. SHE'S BACKING UP!!!!"

* * * * *

Here are a few interesting "did you know" facts about food and eating.
* According to the US Government, people have tried nearly 28,000 different ways to lose weight.
* A raisin that's dropped in a glass of champagne which is still bubbling will bounce up and down.
* Coca-Cola was originally green.
* Babe Ruth wore a cabbage leaf under his cap to keep him cool. He changed it (the cabbage, not the cap), every two innings.
* American Airlines saved $40,000 in 1987 by eliminating one olive from each salad served in first-class.
* Americans eat an average of 18 acres of pizza every day.

*   *   *   *   *

Want to push servers to their limit? Try any of these five things the next time you're at the drive-through window of your favorite fast-food restaurant:
* When you arrive at the window, the server will ask you if s/he can take your order. Act thoroughly snooty, tell him or her you're just window-shopping, and drive away.
* This one works great around Halloween. Your server might ask if you would like ketchup with your order. If that happens, laugh demonically and adopt a thoroughly bizarre smile. Drooling helps too!
* Want to make your server thoroughly crazy? Ask him or her to use the bathroom.
* Tell the server you're on a diet. Then order a cup of water, a napkin, and nothing else.

* When your server hands you your food, hand him/her a bag with all the trash from your car in it.

* * * * *

A true story: realizing that pets need to eat too, Jackie Zajac and Sheila Mullan opened *Fido's Fast Food* in Toledo, Ohio in June of 1992. Pet owners can pick up cheeseburgers, french fries, and peanut butter bagels, which are all dried. For dessert, they can get—among other things—catnip and people-shaped crackers.

* * * * *

No Dough-King: The Pillsbury Doughboy is Dead at 71
With a heavy heart, a Pillsbury official announced that well-known spokesman, The Pillsbury Doughboy, died recently of complications caused by repeated pokes to the belly. He was 73.

The funeral of Doughboy, buried in a lightly greased coffin, attracted dozens of celebrities, including Betty Crocker, the Hostess Twinkies, Captain Crunch, the California Raisins, and Mrs. Butterworth.

Longtime friend Aunt Jemima delivered the eulogy, describing Doughboy as "a man who never knew how much he was kneaded."

Doughboy, who rose quickly in show business, was not considered a very smart cookie. He spent much of his hard-earned dough on half-baked schemes. Nevertheless, he was a roll model for millions, even when a crusty old man.

Doughboy is survived by his second wife, Play Dough. They have two children and another in the oven. The funeral was held at 3:50 for about 20 minutes.

* * * * *

How can you tell when food in your fridge has gone bad?

* Apply the gag test. Any food in your fridge that makes you gag is probably spoiled.
* If something starts pecking its way out of the shell, the egg should take a one-way trip to the trash.
* Milk is past its prime when it starts to look like yogurt. Yogurt is ready to retire when it starts to look like cottage cheese. Cottage cheese should be tossed when it starts to look like regular cheese.
* Frozen foods you have to pry out of the freezer with a knife should be sent to the trash.
* It's probably a safe bet that your meat is spoiled if opening the refrigerator door causes stray animals from a three-block radius to congregate outside your house.
* Don't try to eat lettuce you can't get off the bottom of the vegetable crisper without steel wool.
* If you can tie bows with your carrots, they're probably not fresh.
* Edible potatoes don't have roots or branches.
* If you can take chip dip out of its container and bounce it on the floor, you don't want to eat it.

* * * * *

Let's finish this chapter by looking at what three well-known people have said about food and eating.

* I won't eat anything that has intelligent life, but I'd gladly eat a network executive or a politician.

—Marty Feldman

* My whole life revolves around dessert.

—Marvin Hamlisch

*   I have gained and lost the same ten pounds so many times over and over again that my cellulite must have *deja vu*.

—Jane Wagner

Gender Benders

---◆---

Not long ago, I thought about writing a book that detailed everything men and women know about each other. But then I thought a book that was only one word long—"nothing"—wouldn't sell too well. I figured, though, that there was no better place to write about that joke we call the relationship between men and women than in a collection of humor. Enjoy!

* * * * *

Let's start by acknowledging that there are some things that only women understand.

- * Why it's important to have no fewer than five pairs of black shoes.
- * The difference between cream, ivory, and off-white.
- * Crying can be fun.
- * Guys can buy things, but only women know how to **SSSSHHHHOOOOPPPP!!!!**
- * Fat clothes (Well, not clothing that's overweight—apparel for when people feel that way!).

* A salad, diet drink, and a hot fudge sundae make a balanced lunch.
* Why discovering a designer dress on the clearance rack can be considered a peak life experience.
* The inaccuracy of every bathroom scale ever made.
* A good man might be hard to find, but a good hairdresser is almost non-existent.
* Why a phone call between two women—even a wrong number—can never last fewer than ten minutes.

And the number one thing only a woman can understand:
* **OTHER WOMEN!**

* * * * *

Want to understand man-speak? Maybe this guide will help.
* When a guy says: "I'm going fishing,"
* He actually means: "I'm going to drink myself dangerously stupid, and stand by a stream with a stick in my hand, while the fish swim by in complete safety."

* When a guy says: "Can I help with dinner?"
* He actually means: "Why isn't it already on the table?"

* When a guy says: "uh huh" or "Yes, dear,"
* He actually means: Absolutely nothing. It's a conditioned response.

- When a guy says: "It would take too long to explain,"
- He actually means: "I have no idea how it works."

- When a guy says: "That's really interesting, dear."
- He actually means:"Are you still talking?"

- When a guy says: "Take a break honey. You're working too hard."
- He actually means: "I can't hear the game over the vacuum cleaner."

- When a guy says: "I have a terrible memory."
- He actually means: "I remember the theme song to *F Troop*, the address of the first girl I kissed, and the license numbers of every car I've ever owned, but I forgot your birthday."

- When a guy says: "Oh, it's no big deal. I just cut myself. I'll be fine."
- He actually means: "I have severed a limb, but I will bleed to death before I'll admit that I'm hurt."

- When a guy says: "I've got my reasons for what I'm doing."
- He actually means: "I sure hope I think of some pretty soon."

- When a guy says: "I heard you."
- He actually means: "I don't have any idea what you just said, and I hope I can fake it well enough that you don't spend the next three days yelling at me."

* When a guy says: "You know I could never love anyone else."
* He actually means: "I'm used to the way you yell at me, and realize it could be a lot worse."

* When a guy says: "You look great."
* He actually means: "Oh, God, please don't try on one more outfit. I'm starving."

* When a guy says: "I'm not lost at all."
* He actually means: "No one will ever see us alive again."

* When a guy says: "We share the housework."
* He actually means: "I make the messes, she cleans them up."

* When a guy says: "I can't find it."
* He actually means: "It didn't fall into my outstretched hands, so I'm completely clueless."

* When a guy says: "It's a guy thing."
* He actually means: "There is no rational thought pattern connected to it, and you have no chance at all of making sense of it."

* * * * *

Translating woman-speak can be pretty tricky too. This brief guide should at least help you understand the basics of this very-foreign language.

* When a woman says: "We need…"
* She actually means: "I want…"

* When a woman says: "It's your decision"
* She actually means: "But you already know I'm right"

* When a woman says: "Do whatever you want to do"
* She actually means: "You'll pay for this later"

* When a woman says: "I'm not upset"
* She actually means" I'm furious, you bonehead."

* When a woman says "You're so manly"
* She actually means "You really need a shower and a shave"

* When a woman says "This closet is getting really full."
* She actually means "I want a new house."

* When a woman says "The trash is full."
* She actually means "Empty it."

* When a woman says "We need new curtains"
* She actually means "We need new curtains, and carpeting, and wall-paper. and furniture, and…"

* When a woman says "Just give me a second and I'll be ready"
* She actually means "I'll be ready in about an hour and a half"

* When a woman says "Nothing's wrong"
* She actually means "I'm going to kill you!"

* * * * *

Want to send a man back to school? Here are some training courses he might benefit from.
* The Mop and Sponge Aren't Aliens
* Refrigerator Forensics: Identifying and Removing the Dead
* Accepting Loss: If It's Empty, You Can Throw It Away
* Are Your 1970's Polyester Shirts Hideous?
* Dressing Up: Beyond the Funeral and the Wedding
* A Course in Non-Miracles: The Dishes Won't Wash Themselves
* Just Because You Have Power Tools Doesn't Mean You Can Fix It
* Pretty as a Picture: Sharing the Remote

* * * * *

There are also some really helpful courses for women.
* Silence: A Frontier No Woman Has Ever Explored
* Parties & Weddings: You Don't Need New Outfits To Go
* The Man in Your Life Needs Bathroom Cabinet Space Too
* Tears as the Last Resort, Not the First
* Thinking Before Speaking

* Basic Telephone Skills: Hanging Up
* How Not to Inflict Your Diets on Other People
* Compliments: Accepting Them Gracefully
* Oil and Gas: Your Car Needs Both
* Getting What You Want Without Nagging

* * * * *

There's been a lot of talk lately about being "Politically Correct" when you speak, If that were extended to how people talk about women, we might run into expressions like this:

Traditional Language	Politically-Correct Alternative
BLEACHED BLONDE	PEROXIDE-DEPENDENT
A BAD COOK	MICROWAVE-COMPATIBLE
WEARS TOO MUCH JEWELRY	IS METALLICALLY OVERBURDENED
BIG SHOPPER	MALL-FLUENT
HAS A MUSTACHE	IS IN TOUCH WITH HER MASCULINE SIDE

* * * * *

Ever wonder why someone would want to be a male rather than a female? Here are a few reasons.
* Men's phone conversations often end in fewer than 20 minutes.
* Men can go on vacation for a week and take only one suitcase.

* Men's conversations almost never center around weight loss or gain.
* Men can browse TV channels without pausing to look at every shot of someone crying.
* Men don't have to lug a purse full of "stuff" with them everywhere they go.
* Men can leave a hotel bed unmade.
* Men get extra credit for even the tiniest act of thoughtfulness.
* Men can be showered and ready in ten minutes.
* Men's co-workers can't make them cry.
* Men can be 33 and single and no one will comment on it.
* Men don't worship at the Church of Chocolate. For them, chocolate is just another snack.
* Men know flowers fix everything.
* Men are convinced two pairs of shoes are more than enough.
* Men don't feel the need to clean their apartments if they know the meter reader is coming by.
* Men are told the truth by car mechanics.
* Men can get a haircut and not give a damn if no one notices.
* Men can watch a game with a friend in total silence and not think "He must be mad at me."
* Men with gray hair and wrinkles have character.
* Men don't worry that someone is talking about them behind their backs.
* Men don't have to convince others to share their desserts with them.

* Men can drop by to see a friend without having to bring a little gift.
* Men have relatively normal relationships with their mothers.
* Men can buy shoes that don't mangle their feet.
* Men don't have to remember everyone's birthdays and anniversaries.

* * * * *

At the same time, though, there are plenty of good reasons to be a woman. Here are just a few.

* Women can get free meals and drinks.
* Women can buy new lipstick and get a whole new lease on life.
* Women will never face a fashion *faux pas* to rival The Speedo®.
* Women know that true excitement is only as far away as the nearest beauty-supply store.
* Women never have to punch holes through anything with their fists.
* Women can end any fight quickly and easily by crying.
* Women never have to live down having had a goatee.
* Women know which glass is theirs because of the lipstick mark.
* Women know there are times when chocolate can solve all their problems.

* * * * *

What about men and women who decide to tie the knot? Here a few funny and thought-provoking quotations on the subject.

* "A man is incomplete until he is married. After that, he is finished."
    —Zsa Zsa Gabor

* " I recently read that love is entirely a matter of chemistry. That must be why my wife treats me like toxic waste."
    —David Bissonette

* "I've sometimes thought of marrying, and then I've thought again."
    —Noel Coward

* "When a man steals your wife, there is no better revenge than to let him keep her."
    —Sacha Guitry

* "She's a lovely person. She deserves a good husband. Marry her before she finds one."
    —Oscar Levant to Harpo Marx upon meeting Harpo's fiancee

* "After marriage, husband and wife become two sides of a coin: they can't face each other, but still they stay together."
    —Hemant Joshi

* A successful man is one who makes more money than his wife can spend. A successful woman is one who can find such a man.
    —Lana Turner

* Marriage is a great institution, but I'm not ready for an institution.
    —Mae West

* "I was married by a judge…I should have asked for a jury."
    —George Burns

The following were said by someone named "Anonymous."

* "Marriage is a three ring circus: engagement ring, wedding ring, and suffering."
* "Marriage is bliss. Ignorance is bliss. Therefore…"
* "Marriage is not a word; it's a sentence."
* "Marriage is when a man and woman become as one; the trouble starts when they try to decide which one."
* "Marriages are made in heaven. But then again, so are thunder and lightning."
* "I had some words with my wife, and she had some paragraphs with me."
* "If you want your spouse to listen and pay strict attention to every word you say, talk in your sleep."
* "Behind every successful man stands an amazed Mother-in-Law!"

* * * * *

Want to draw a conclusion about the relationship between men and women? Consider this comment from Rebecca West:

"The main difference between men and women is that men are lunatics and women are idiots."

Just For The Health Of It

◆

Going to the hospital or seeing a doctor can be pretty scary. But the medical world can also provide lots of laughs. I hope this "prescription" helps you.

* * * * *

Let's start things off with a true story. A mother and her two daughters, ages six and two, went to the dentist for a check up. The older daughter was being examined by the dentist, and the two-year-old, in the waiting room with her mother, kept herself occupied by playing with her toys. The mother, meanwhile, was resting, and had her eyes closed. The two-year-old marched up to her mother, and said in a voice loud enough to be heard by the six other patients in the waiting room: "Mommy, wake up! This is not church!"

* * * * *

Mrs. Hughes, who was an older woman, woke up one morning with a nasty case of hiccups. So she went to see a doctor. The doctor examined her and said she was pregnant. Mrs. Hughes freaked out, screamed, and ran out of the clinic at full speed.

Soon afterwards, the doctor—with a big smile on his face—told one of his partners what had happened. "What's the matter with you?" the partner asked. "Mrs. Hughes is 67 years old. There's no way she could be pregnant."

The doctor's grinning reply? "Cured her of her hiccups, though, didn't I?"

* * * * *

Snow White has been rewritten. There are only six dwarves this time, though, because Doc got replaced by an HMO.

* * * * *

Speaking of HMO's, here are a few HMO-related questions and the answers to them.

Q: What does HMO stand for?

A: Some people think HMO is an abbreviation for "Health Maintenance Organization." But it's actually shorthand for "Hey, Moe!" in honor of Moe Howard of *The Three Stooges* fame. Howard discovered that a patient would forget about his back pain if he was poked hard enough in the eyes. Things have changed a little since Moe's day—we now have expensive tests, new surgical techniques, pricey prescriptions, and HMO's to provide pain instead of poking people in the eye.

Q: Do HMO's require pre-certification for all diagnostic procedures?
A: No. Only the ones you need.

Q: I just joined an HMO. Can I choose the doctor I want?
A: When you signed up, your HMO most likely gave you a book that listed all the doctors you could see. There's probably only one doctor left in the plan who's still accepting new patients, but don't worry—her office is only half a day's drive away.

Q: What about alternative forms of medicine?
A: HMO's require that you find alternative forms of payment for them.

Q: What if I get sick while traveling?
A: Try sitting in a different part of the bus.

Q: No, I mean what should I do if I'm away from home and get sick?
A: Don't do that. Seeing your primary care physician would be really tough. Wait until you come home and get sick then.

Q: My HMO's pharmacy plan only covers generic drugs, but I need the name brand. Generic medications give me a headache. What should I do?
A: Poke yourself in the eye.

* * * * *

Another great source of medical madness is the typographical transgressions, weird writing, and spelling slip-ups found on medical charts and reports. Here are a few actual ones.

* The patient has been depressed ever since she began seeing me in 1993.
* The baby was delivered, the cord clamped and cut, and handed to the pediatrician, who breathed and cried immediately.
* The skin was moist and dry.
* The patient had waffles for breakfast and anorexia for lunch.
* I saw your patient today, who is still under our car for physical therapy.
* The patient lives at home with his mother, father, and pet turtle, who is presently enrolled in day care three times a week.
* She is numb from her toes down.
* While in the emergency room, she was examined, x-rated, and sent home.
* The patient suffers from occasional, constant, infrequent headaches.
* Coming from Detroit, this man has no children.
* Patient has chest pain if she lies on her left side for over a year.
* On the 2nd day the knee was better and on the 3rd day it disappeared completely.
* Patient has two teenage children, but no other abnormalities.

* * * * *

The following comments, questions, and exchanges actually happened when a doctor had to testify in a court .

- "Now doctor, isn't it true that when a person dies in his sleep, he doesn't know about it until the next morning?"
- "The youngest son, the twenty-year-old, how old is he?"
- "Doctor, before you performed the autopsy, did you check for a pulse?"

"No."

"Did you check for blood pressure?"

"No."

"Did you check for breathing?"

"No."

"So, then it is possible that the patient was alive when you began the autopsy?"

"No."

"How can you be so sure, Doctor?"

"Because his brain was sitting on my desk in a jar."

"But could the patient have still been alive nevertheless?"

"It is possible that he could have been alive and practicing law somewhere."

* * * * *

RING
RING
CLICK

Voice Mail—"Hello, Welcome to the Psychiatric Hotline. Callers who are obsessive-compulsive should press one repeatedly. Callers who are co-dependent, please ask someone to press two. Callers who have multiple personalities should press three, four, five, and six. Callers who are paranoid-delusional—we know who you are and what you want. Your call is being traced. Callers who are schizophrenic should listen carefully—the voices in your head will tell you which number to press. Callers who are manic-depressive: it doesn't matter which number you press. No one will answer."

* * * * *

There's all sorts of specific language in the medical world. If someone with less-than-optimum brain-power wrote a dictionary of medical terms, would it look like this?

Word	Definition
Artery	Study of paintings
Bacteria	Back door of a cafeteria
Benign	The age you be after you be eight
Caesarean section	A district in Rome
Cat scan	Searching for a kitty
Cauterize	Made eye contact with a woman
Coma	A punctuation mark
Dilate	Live a long time
Enema	Opposite of "friend"
Fester	Quicker
Fibula	A really small lie
G.I. Series	A group of baseball games played by soldiers
Hangnail	A hook people put their coats on
Impotent	Significant

Labor pain	Being hurt at work
Medical staff	Doctor's cane
Morbid	Higher offer
Nitrate	Takes effect after 5 p.m.
Node	Past tense of "Know that"
Outpatient	Any patient who faints
Pelvis	Elvis impersonator
Post-operative	Letter carrier
Protein	Favoring adolescents
Recovery room	A place where upholstery is treated
Rheumatic	Affectionate
Seizure	Well-known Roman emperor
Serology	The study of knighthood
Tablet	Small table
Tibia	A country in Asia
Tumor	An extra pair
Varicose	Not distant at all
Vein	Cocky

* * * * *

No matter how well you take care of yourself, the time will probably come when you have to have some surgery done. Just pray your doctor never says any of these during the operation:

- * "Someone should call the janitor—we'll need a mop."
- * "Wait a minute Spot! Come back with that!"
- * "I'm confused. If that's her spleen, what's this thingie?"

* "Shoot—there go the lights again."
* "Stand back everyone! I just lost my contact lens!"
* "Neat, huh? Now watch me make his leg twitch."
* "Oh, darn: I forgot my glasses."
* "Now where did I leave that scalpel?"
* "Don't worry. That's sharp enough."
* "He's gonna blow—everyone hit the floor!"
* " I can't find that doggone manual."

* * * * *

Well-known heart specialist Dr. Michael DeBakey was having some trouble with his car, so he took it in to get it fixed. The repair was pretty simple: DeBakey's car just needed some new valves. The mechanic, who was a bit of a loud-mouth, went to work. He also said to DeBakey "we do pretty much the same thing, ya know—I'm going to take the valves out and put new ones in. Just like you. But I wonder: why do I get such lousy pay and you get big bucks for doing essentially the same thing as me?"

DeBakey didn't want to get into an extended conversation with the guy, so he walked to the station's waiting room. Before he left, though, he said to the mechanic—"Try doing your work with the engine running."

* * * * *

Do you think doctors don't use humor on the job? Here's a true story that might cure you of any thoughts like that.

A man was about to be wheeled into the operating room for hernia surgery, and decided to have a little fun. So he taped a magazine picture of a well-muscled male torso to his stomach and included a note for the surgeon that said "Dear Dr. Debby: Desired results, please."

After the operation, the man awoke in his room and saw that the doctor had given him an impressive set of "abs"—drawn on his abdomen with a felt-tipped marker.

*   *   *   *   *

To remind you that the final stages of pregnancy can be almost as stressful for men as women, I offer another true story.

A man was married to a woman who'd begun having labor pains. The husband called the doctor and told him "My wife is pregnant and her contractions are only two minutes apart!"

"Is this her first child?" the doctor asked.

"No, you idiot!" the man shouted, "This is her husband!"

*   *   *   *   *

Are you confused sometimes by what your doctor tells you? Well, I provided a trans-lation guide for guytalk and womanspeak, so I should help you translate doctor dialogue.

- * If your doc says: "This should be taken care of right away."
- * S/he actually means: "I'm going on a vacation to Hawaii next month, and this easy and totally unnecessary operation would be a great way to pay for it."

* If your doc says: "Let me check your medical history."
* S/he actually means: "I want to look at your file and see if you paid your last bill before I spend any more time with you."

* If your doc says: "Let's make another appointment for you later in the week after I talk with my colleagues."
* S/he actually means: "I really need the bucks, and I want to charge you for another office visit."

* If your doc says: "Let me schedule you for some tests."
* S/he actually means: "I have a thirty-five percent interest in the lab."

* If your doc says: "If it doesn't clear up in a week, give me a call."
* S/he actually means: "I have no idea what it is, and I sure hope it will go away by itself."

* If your doc says: "Everything seems to be normal."
* S/he actually means: "Darn! I guess I'd better not buy that condo after all."

* If your doc says: "This might hurt a bit."
* S/he actually means: "Last week two patients I did it to screamed and bit off their tongues."

* If your doc says: "Perhaps you're feeling stress"
* S/he actually means: "Man, you're totally crazy. I sure hope I can find a shrink who'll give me a big referral fee."

* * * * *

It's a bit unnerving that doctors call what they do "practice."

* * * * *

Time is a great healer. That's why we spend so long in the waiting room when we go to see our doctors.

* * * * *

A man went to see his doctor for his annual physical, and told the doc he couldn't do all the things around the house that he used to do. When the examination was finished, the man said "Tell me the truth in plain English doc. What's wrong with me."

"In plain English," said the doctor, "you're just lazy."

"Okay," the man replied. "Now I need the totally confusing medical term for it so I can tell my wife."

* * * * *

Lots of health hilarity can be found in letters to welfare. Here are excerpts from a few of the strangest letters welfare has ever received.

* I am writing the welfare department to say that my baby was born two years old. When do I get my money?

* I cannot get sick pay. I have six children. Can you tell me why?
* This is my eighth child. What are you going to do about it?
* I am forwarding my marriage certificate and my three children, one of which is a mistake as you can see.
* Unless I get my husband's money pretty soon, I will be forced to lead an immortal life.
* You have changed my little boy to a girl. Will this make any difference?
* In accordance with your instructions, I have given birth to twins in the enclosed envelope.

* * * * *

We started this chapter with a true story. Let's finish with another one.

A woman who's both a physician and a mother was driving her then-four-year-old daughter to preschool one day. The doctor had left her stethoscope on the car seat, and her daughter picked it up and started playing with it. The mother was delighted, because she thought this meant her daughter wanted to follow in Mommy's footsteps and become a doctor. Nope! The child treated the stethoscope like a microphone and said "Welcome to McDonald's. May I take your order?"

Say What?

♦

Because my brain tumor left me deaf, I have a special interest in issues that are hearing-related. I've learned that life without all or part of your hearing can be really tough at times. It can also be really funny too. I hope this chapter offers you some laughs, giggles, and smiles.

I have a secret dream, and I need your help to make it come true. I want to put together a book of hearing-related humor. I know there are lots of true stories about hearing (or the lack of it, I guess) out there. and I'd love to get some of the material for the book from readers of **He Who Laughs Lasts**. So if you've had a personal (and amusing) experience with life sans hearing, or someone you know has, send it to me. You can e-mail it to me at lovley@erols.com—or mail it to me in care of the publisher. Thanks a bunch!

Since that book is somewhere in the distant future (is that a sigh of relief I "hear" from you?), I thought I'd better include some hearing-related humor in **He Who Laughs Lasts**. So here's some of the best I've ever run across.

*   *   *   *   *

During South Africa's Boer War the situation on the front lines was very tense. One day, the commanding officer summoned a hard-of-hearing soldier and told him to take this message to headquarters: "Send reinforcements, we are going to advance."

The hard-of-hearing guy nodded his head and ran to headquarters. He then relayed his commander's orders—or at least what he thought he'd heard:

"Send four and six pence, we're going to a dance."

*   *   *   *   *

A man had lost some of his hearing as he grew older, so he decided to get hearing aids. He went to his audiologist, had his hearing tested, and ordered a pair of top-of-the-line aids. They arrived two weeks later.

After wearing them for about a month, the man returned to his audiologist for a check-up. The audiologist asked the man how he liked his new hearing aids. "They're wonderful," came the reply. "I can hear so much more now that I have them. It's so nice to hear everything my family says."

"I bet your wife and family are really happy you got them, too" said the audiologist.

"Oh I haven't told them about the hearing aids yet," the man replied, "but I have changed my will three times since I got them!"

*   *   *   *   *

Another older, hard-of-hearing guy went to see his doctor for his annual physical. Tests showed there were no major problems. The doctor offered the man some quick advice, and sent him on his way.

A little while later, the doctor saw the man walking down the street with his arm around a beautiful young woman and wearing a big smile on his face.

At the man's next appointment, the doctor said to the guy, "You look great. Any words of wisdom for the world?"

The man smiled and said "I'm just doing what you said, Doc, You told me to get a hot mama and be cheerful."

"Actually" replied the doctor. "what I said was that you've got a heart murmur and should be careful."

*   *   *   *   *

Three hard-of-hearing guys were sitting together outside, enjoying the beautiful weather. In an effort to strike up a conversation, which had been sorely lacking, one remarked "Boy, it sure is windy today." The second replied. "No, I think it's Thursday." The third then added "Yeah, I'm thirsty too. Let's go get a drink."

*   *   *   *   *

In closed-captioned movies and television shows, the words of the performers appear in text at the bottom or top of the screen so a viewer can read them instead of hearing what's said. As you can imagine, I love captions.

One day a few months ago, I was doing my standard exercise routine, and in a desperate attempt to make the time go by faster, I was watching TV while I worked out—specifically, a talk show that's broadcasted live. Watching live TV means you see exactly what happens on the show when it actually takes place. There's no editing or time delay at all. The same is true of captioning. Sometimes that leads to hysterical captioning boo-boos. While watching the show, I saw a captioning blooper that was both hilarious and frightening.

One of the guests on the show started talking about cooking, and a recipe he was particularly fond of, which called for Parmesan cheese. Except the caption didn't read "Parmesan." It said "pair Shawn."

Two of me? Definitely a scary thought! As my wonderful wife said after I told her about the real-o and we'd stopped laughing about it: "I don't know if I could handle two of you. One is plenty."

* * * * *

I also love subtitles, since they allow me to read words instead of having to figure out what was said and then try to translate it. Occasionally, they provide some real hilarity too. This is particularly true when the person writing the subtitles isn't totally fluent in English and has trouble translating the spoken words. Here are just a few of the more bizarre subtitles I've run across. Saying "huh?" is definitely permitted.

* Take my advice, or I'll spank you without pants.
* Fatty, you with your thick face have hurt my instep.
* A normal person wouldn't steal pituitaries.
* You always use violence. I should've ordered glutinous rice chicken.
* Damn, I'll burn you into a BBQ chicken!
* Quiet or I'll blow your throat up.
* You daring lousy guy.
* The bullets inside are very hot. Why do I feel so cold?
* How can you use my intestines as a gift?

* * * * *

There are also all sorts of funny and true stories about life without hearing. Here are just a few of the best ones I've ever "heard."

My friend Alan Sprague, who lost his hearing several years ago, e-mailed me a story about a voice call he got recently. I get them all the time, but this one struck me as especially funny. I hope it makes you laugh as hard as I did when Alan shared it with me.

One evening (at dinner time, of course) a telemarketer called the Spragues. Alan's college-age son, James, who's hearing, answered. The voice on the other end said: "This is the Acme Carpet Cleaning Company. May I speak to Mr. Sprague, please?"

James did what he usually does when his dad gets voice calls: he said something like "I'm sorry, he's hearing-impaired and can't hear on the phone. May I take a message?"

Voice: "Um, no that's ok, I'll call him back later."

James: "Well, unfortunately he'll still be deaf later, so if you'd like to leave a message for him I'll pass it on."

Voice: "Well, that's ok, deaf people don't need their carpets cleaned anyway."

James questioned that inane comment, and the caller hung up.

James was miffed and disturbed, so he grabbed the phone book and looked up the number of the Acme Carpet Cleaning Company. He called the company, and the phone was answered by the person who had just called.

James: "May I speak to the owner or manager, please?"

Voice: "Sorry, he's not in. May I take a message?"

James: "Yes, tell him I wish to speak to him regarding his telephone sales program."

Voice: "Oh. Uh, we have no phone sales program."

James: "Ok, fine. Please give me the company mailing address."

Voice: "Well, I don't know what it is, sorry." Click

James checked the phone book and found the company's address easily. He wrote a short letter to the owner complaining about the caller.

A couple evenings later the owner called the Spragues and claimed the caller was simply a temporary worker who was no longer with the company. "But we'd still like to clean your carpets for you," the owner said. "And we'll give you a discount."

James replied: "Well thanks, that's very nice of you. But deaf people don't need their carpets cleaned." Click.

* * * * *

Limited hearing can wreak real havoc on romance. Years ago, a hard-of-hearing woman was having a great time at a dance with a handsome young man. She was wearing her hearing aids, and in what should have been the middle of all the fun, the batteries stopped working. So she told the young man her batteries were dead—and didn't say that she meant her hearing aid batteries. Just imagine how baffled and depressed the young man must have felt!

* * * * *

The expression "deaf and dumb" has become less and less common over the years, having been replaced by terms like "deaf or hard-of-hearing," "hearing-impaired" and the like. There are times, though, when the expression "deaf and dumb" is still used. A t-shirt I saw recently shows that the term can be a source of great guffaws. Worn by a deafened woman when she goes out walking with her husband, it says: (On the front) "I Am Deaf" (On the back, with an arrow pointing right) "He's Dumb."

* * * * *

A deaf man was staying in a hotel on business and needed a wake-up call so he could make it to an early morning flight home. He stopped at the hotel desk the night before he was supposed to leave, and very carefully explained that he was deaf and would need someone to come into his room and wake him up the following morning since he wouldn't be able to hear the phone ring.

Things didn't quite work out that way, though. The following morning, the deaf guy awoke about an hour after he was supposed to be woken up. He ran around trying to get ready in time to make his plane. He did really well, and after he'd gotten dressed and finished a little last-minute packing, he headed for the door. That's when he noticed a note stuck on his TV that said: "Time to get up!"

* * * * *

My friend Carolyn is extremely hard-of-hearing, and wears a cochlear implant to help her hear better. She also likes to do walking meditation on her narrow country roads. In order to focus better on clearing her mind, she doesn't wear her cochlear implant when she's doing walking meditation. In the winter, she often pulls her hat 'way down to block out all sight other than the road beneath her feet.

One winter day after a light snow storm, she did just that. She was deep in concentration when—about a half hour into her walk—she felt a strong vibration beneath her feet. She looked up. Perched high above the ground, in her town's biggest plow-truck, was a driver with an expression of extreme frustration on his face. He was very carefully keeping pace with her slow walk, moving his plow forward inch by tortured inch.

* * * * *

A deafened mother told me she wasn't a very good mom in many ways. For example, she usually left attending her kids' music recitals to her hearing husband. The last time she went to one, though, she was determined to pay attention and at least try to look interested.

When the playing began, she stared with resolve at the stage. The children put down their instruments, and the woman burst into applause. But no one else was clapping. The antennae that most deaf folks have reared its head, and knowing she had misstepped somehow, the woman turned to her husband, who was watching her with a look of rather horrified interest. "Sweetie," he said, making sure she could understand every word, "they just finished playing a practice scale."

* * * * *

A deaf woman became worried about her cat, who was acting very strangely.

Usually very vivacious and playful, the feline now cowered in a corner in the very back of her house, as far from the kitchen as she could get, for most of the day. Puzzled, the woman took the animal to the vet, who could find nothing wrong with it. When the woman and the feline got home again, though, the cat ran as fast as possible to its hiding place.

Wanting to get her mind off her worries, the woman decided to give her house a good cleaning. She didn't often use her vacuum cleaner, since she had wood floors. But she decided to give the entire house a vacuuming this time. Opening the door of the spare room where she stowed her vacuum cleaner, she solved the mystery of her cat's "illness." The woman's very noisy vacuum cleaner was sitting there, going full blast—just as it had been since she used it the week before.

* * * * *

A good friend lost most of her hearing a few years back, and wears a cochlear implant (CI) now—most of the time, that is. The following true story tells one really scary thing that can happen when a implant-wearer goes C.I.-less.

One day she was hard at work sewing in the back room of her house. She always removes her CI when she sews, and had also taken off her glasses this time so she could look very closely at a seam she was mending. With the family dog asleep at her feet, she was having a totally calm day.

That didn't last for long, though. She looked up suddenly and (hazily, because she's very nearsighted) saw two men, who thrust their arms towards her and shined a light in her eyes. She screamed, stood up, tripped over the dog, and began to babble "What is it? What is it? Where are my eyes?"

She located her glasses quickly and saw that two policemen stood in front of her. My friend, who says she's not known for grace under pressure, started to yell things like: "Oh my God, my son" because her oldest had just begun driving himself to school. and "Oh my God my mother," since she has a mother in a nursing home. "Where are my e...a.....rrr..s?"

The police were (to put it mildly) a bit taken aback by the crazy woman in front of them, so they backed up a step or two. My friend, seeing she wasn't about to be shot on the spot, calmed down a bit, found her CI, and began to unravel what had happened.

Alone in the house without her CI on, she hadn't heard two Jehovah's Witnesses knock on her door earlier. For some reason, they had peered in a window, and had seen a message that her youngest son had posted on the window years ago as part of a game. It said "Help me." Taking the command to heart, the two Witnesses jumped in their car, drove to a nearby store, and called the police to report a hostage situation.

When the police arrived, they also got no response to their knocking. So the cops let themseves in. Guns were drawn and flashlights were turned on, in preparation for a nasty confrontation with one really scary person.

*   *   *   *   *

My friend Lynsie is late-deafened, and about a year after they were married, she and her husband bought their first house. They realized they had a problem in terms of his letting her know when he had come home, but solved it easily: he would flash the lights in the entryway when he arrived, and she would see it and know it was him.

That worked really well. But one day things took a strange twist. The wife was taking a shower when the husband came home, and he wanted to let her know he was home so she wouldn't be unduly surprised. So the husband reached for the light switch in the bathroom to flick it off and on. Unfortunately, just as the man inserted his hand through a crack in the door, his wife pulled the shower curtain back and saw it. She screamed and reached for the nearest weapon at hand—which happened to be an open bottle of shampoo—and heaved it at the door, just as it opened all the way. Fortunately, her husband has always looked good in green, because he was instantly coated with green shampoo from forehead to chest.

Color Me ~~Blue~~ Blonde

◆

One of the most prolific sources of humor is joking about blonde-haired peo-ple. Blondes supposedly aren't—to put it mildly—too bright. My wife and I are both blonde, and while I know (hope?) there's no truth to the idea that blonde people lack smarts, I still find myself laughing hysterically at humor having to do with people with saffron locks. I hope you do the same when you read the following.

* * * * *

Did you hear about the blonde who sent a friend a fax with a stamp on it?

* * * * *

You know a blonde office-mate has been sending e-mail if you see a bunch of envelopes stuffed into her disk drive.

* * * * *

How about the blonde who thought a quarterback was a 25-cent rebate?

* * * * *

Then there was the blonde who put lipstick on her forehead because she wanted to make up her mind.

* * * * *

One blonde took a ruler to bed to see how long she slept.

* * * * *

Another told a friend to meet her at the corner of "WALK" and "DON'T WALK."

* * * * *

A blonde filled out an application, and where it said "sign here" wrote "Aries."

* * * * *

Then there was a blonde who made an appointment for a blood test and started studying.

* * * * *

A blonde was driving to the airport recently and saw a sign that said "AIRPORT LEFT." She turned around and went home.

* * * * *

Did you hear about the blonde who spent 20 minutes staring at an orange juice container because it said "concentrate?"

* * * * *

One had to put "TGIF" on her shoes to remind her "Toes Go In First."

* * * * *

Another burned her nose bobbing for French fries.

* * * * *

There's one sure sign a blonde has been making chocolate chip cookies. You find M&M shells all over the kitchen floor.

* * * * *

Speaking of M&M's, you can drive a blonde crazy really easily with them. Just give her a bag of M&M's and ask her to alphabetize them.

* * * * *

Here's one more joke about blondes and M&M's. A blonde used to work at the M&M factory—as a proofreader—but she was fired because she kept throwing out the W's.

* * * * *

Did you hear about the blonde who fell out of a tree while raking leaves?

* * * * *

What about the blonde who couldn't make ice cubes because she lost the recipe?

* * * * *

Another kitchen-impaired blonde refused to buy TV dinners because she didn't know what channel to cook them on.

* * * * *

Two blondes were walking down the street, and one noticed a compact someone had dropped. She picked it up, opened it, looked in the mirror, and said to her companion "Hmm, that person looks familiar." Her pal seized the compact, looked in the mirror, and said "You airhead. That's me!"

* * * * *

A while ago, a blonde entered the ranks of the employed. One of her first assignments was to go out and buy coffee for all her office-mates. She grabbed a thermos and headed for the local coffee emporium. She arrived, and a clerk came over to take her order. The blonde held up the thermos. "Is this big enough to hold six cups of coffee?" she asked. "Looks it," came the reply. "Oh, good," said the blonde. "I'd like two regular, two black, and two decaf."

* * * * *

For some people, alligator shoes are the height of fashion. They can also be very expensive. But a blonde was determined to get a pair and save some serious money too. So she went to Louisiana for vacation, and as soon as she arrived, headed for the countryside to do some alligator hunting. She did well, too, bagging six alligators. But after the sixth one, the blonde broke down and cried: "Oh, no! This one isn't wearing any shoes either!"

* * * * *

How are blondes and beer bottles alike? They're both empty from the neck up.

* * * * *

What's the difference between Bigfoot and smart blondes? Bigfoot might exist.

* * * * *

What do you do when a blonde throws a grenade at you? Pull the pin and throw it back.

*　　*　　*　　*　　*

If she throws a pin at you, though, run—she's got a grenade in her mouth.

*　　*　　*　　*　　*

A blonde decided to try horseback riding. She climbed on a horse and it started moving. Everything went great at first, but then the blonde slipped from the saddle. She tried to hold onto the horse's mane, but couldn't get a good grip. Meanwhile, the horse just galloped along, apparently oblivious to the rider's troubles. The blonde tried to leap away from the horse, but her foot had become entangled in the stirrup. So she was at the mercy of the horse. Her head was battered against the ground, and she was on the verge of unconsciousness. But then a hero came to her rescue…the store's manager arrived and shut the horse off.

*　　*　　*　　*　　*

How do you know a blonde has been using your computer? There's white-out on the screen.

*　　*　　*　　*　　*

Any blonde who dyes her hair brown obviously believes in artificial intelligence.

*　　*　　*　　*　　*

Years ago Jimmy Dean starred in a movie called *Rebel Without a Cause*. Hollywood is planning an update—but with a blonde in the lead. The title? *Rebel Without a Clue.*

* * * * *

Ever notice you almost never see blonde pharmacists? That's because they can't get those pesky prescription bottles into typewriters to type the labels.

* * * * *

One morning a blonde called a friend and asked her to come over and help out with a jigsaw puzzle the blonde was having trouble with.

The friend asked "What's it a puzzle of?"

The blonde's response: "There's a picture of a tiger on the box."

The friend said "Okay, I'll be right there." She hung up, and headed over to the blonde's place. The blonde let her in, and showed her the puzzle, which was spread all over the table. The friend looked at the pieces for a moment, then checked out the box. She turned to her blonde pal, and with great sadness in her voice. said:

"Sorry, but I can't help you. I'd suggest you have a cup of coffee, relax, and put all these Frosted Flakes back in the box."

* * * * *

Speaking of puzzles—there were three blondes who went to a bar and asked the bartender for three shots. The blondes got the drinks, and toasted each other with the words "51 days!" They finished their drinks, and asked the bartender for another round. He complied, and again the blondes toasted each other with "51 days!" The bartender was fascinated, and when he'd filled their third order and listened to another "51 days!" toast, he said "You'll have to excuse me ladies, but I'm really curious. Tell me what '51 days' means." So one explained, "We got a jigsaw puzzle almost two months ago. The box said '2-4 years,' and we did it in just 51 days!"

* * * * *

Know why blondes can't dial 911? They can't find the eleven on the phone.

* * * * *

You might wonder why blonde nurses bring red crayons to work. It's in case they have to draw blood.

* * * * *

Need a definition for the term "gross ignorance?" Try "144 blondes."

* * * * *

Know why lots of blondes drive VW's? Because they can't spell "BMW."

* * * * *

What do you call a blonde between two brunettes? A mental block.

* * * * *

Want to make a blonde's eyes twinkle? Just shine a flashlight in her ear.

* * * * *

Did you hear about the blonde who climbed the chain link fence? She wanted to see what was on the other side.

* * * * *

One blonde decided not to make pudding because she couldn't figure out how to get two cups of milk into those little packages.

* * * * *

When a blonde blows in another blonde's ear, it's called "data transfer."

* * * * *

What's a blonde's favorite wine? "Daaaaddy, I want to go to the Bahamas!"

* * * * *

What do you call a blonde who sits in a tree with a brief case? A Branch Manager.

* * * * *

Then there was the blonde who looked into a box of Cheerios and said "Oh look! Doughnut seeds!"

* * * * *

What do you see when you look into a blonde's eyes? The back of her head.

* * * * *

A true story:

In July, 1997, a blonde from Wisconsin was vacationing at a resort on Table Rock Lake in Missouri. It was a hot summer day, and the air conditioners were running in all of the guest cabins.

The blonde came to the door of the owner's living quarters and said, "A fuse just blew in our cabin!"

The owner went to the cabin, and saw that the air conditioner was on. Perfectly normal. But an electric space heater was also turned on—to its maximum output.

The owner was more than a bit perplexed, and asked the blonde why she had both the air conditioner and the electric heater running full blast. The blonde's response? She wanted to shave her legs and it was too cold in the room to do that. So she got the electric heater from her car. Then she said that when she gets cold she gets goose bumps—and that she was afraid she would cut the heads off the goose bumps when she shaved her legs.

* * * * *

One afternoon, a blonde returned from a shopping trip to find her house on fire. She dialed 911 and said "Come quick. My house is on fire." The 911 operator grabbed a pencil and asked the blonde "How do we get there?" The blonde's response? "With a red fire truck."

* * * * *

A blonde wanted to cash a check she'd received, so she went into a bank and stood in front of a teller. "I'd like to cash this check, please" the blond said, handing it to the teller.

The teller examined the check, and said: "Could you please identify yourself, Miss?" The blonde was confused for just a second, then dug around in her handbag, producing a mirror. She glanced in it, and with great relief said, "Yep. That's me, all right!"

* * * * *

Know why the blonde had blisters on her lips? From trying to blow out light-bulbs.

* * * * *

One blonde decided to climb up to the roof of a bar because she heard that the drinks were on the house.

* * * * *

Did you hear about the blonde who wrote "no smoking" on the bottom of her swimming pool?

* * * * *

A blonde who came to Washington, DC, for the first time wanted to see the White House. She knew she'd have to take a bus to get there, but wasn't sure which one. So she asked a police officer for directions.

"Excuse me, officer," the blonde said, "how do I get to the White House?"

The officer responded, "Just wait here for the 54 bus. It'll take you right there." The blonde thanked the officer, and he headed off.

Three hours later the police officer came back to the same area, and the blonde was still standing at the bus stop.

The officer got out of his car and said, "Excuse me, I said to wait here for the number 54 bus, but that was three hours ago. Why are you still waiting?"

The blonde said, "Don't worry, officer, it won't be long now. The 45th bus just went by."

* * * * *

You might have heard about the blonde who bought two copies of the same comic book—in case she wanted to read it twice.

* * * * *

Want to sink a submarine full of blondes? Knock on the door.

* * * * *

What do you call it when three blondes walk into a building? I'm not sure, but you'd think one of them would have seen it.

* * * * *

How do you drive a blonde crazy? Put her in a round room and tell her to stand in the corner.

* * * * *

A cooking-impaired blonde with burnt feet went to see her doctor. "How did you burn your feet?" he asked. "Cooking soup," the blonde replied. "The instructions said 'open can…stand in boiling water for 7 minutes.'"

* * * * *

Did you hear about the blonde who bought a brown cow? She didn't want to keep buying chocolate milk.

* * * * *

A husband was a scout leader. On the weekend of his troop's big camping trip, though, the man became really ill. So his blonde wife Joanne offered to take over for him and lead the troop on the trek. The husband was delighted.

Joanne showed she had some real organizational skills, too—Tina was responsible for bringing the food supplies, Bob was told to handle the cooking, Johnnie was in charge of the maps and drawing up a time schedule for the scouts, and Bert was told to decide what things they would do.

The kids arrived at their campsite. The first order of business was to check out the wildlife in the area. Before the scouts could do that, though, they had to make something to eat. So Bob headed off to start a fire to do the cooking. But in about ten minutes he came back and told

Joanne, "I'm having trouble. Those matches you brought won't light, so we don't have a fire yet."

Joanne was baffled. "I can't understand what's wrong," she said. "Those matches worked fine when I tested them just before we left."

* * * * *

Two women were walking down the road when one of them saw a dog with just one eye. She said, "Look at that dog with one eye!"

Her blonde pal covered one of her eyes and asked, "Where is it?"

* * * * *

A blonde who had just gotten her license entered a passing zone and started driving down the center of the road at almost 95 miles per hour. A police officer pulled the blonde over and told her she was driving recklessly and too fast. "That's okay, Officer," the blonde said. "I have a special license that allows me to drive down the center of the road at really high speeds."

The officer was incredulous. "That's impossible!" he said. "There's no such license."

The blonde knew there was, though, and that she had one. So she reached into her purse and handed the officer her license. The nonplussed cop looked at it and replied: "Just as I suspected. This is an ordinary license. There's nothing on it that would allow you to do what you did."

So the blonde pointed to the bottom of the license and said, "But it says 'Tear On the Dotted Line.'"

* * * * *

(Blonde) Revenge is Sweet

- Why are most blonde jokes so short? So brunettes won't forget them.
- Why are there so many blonde jokes? Because brunettes don't have anything else to do on Saturday nights.
- Brunettes are very proud of their hair color. You know why? Because it matches their mustaches.
- What's the difference between a brunette and the trash? The trash gets taken out at least once a week.
- What's a one-word description of a brunette whose gets a call for a date? Try "startled."
- What do you call a good-looking man with a brunette? A hostage.
- What's black and blue and brown and found in a ditch? A brunette who told too many blonde jokes.

Live and Laugh

No doubt about it; sometimes the only sense you can make of life is a sense of humor. The next time you're ready to scream at life, try laughing instead. If that's hard to do, maybe reading (or **re**-reading, I hope) this chapter will help.

* * * * *

For starters, ask yourself if life is stressing you out. While it can be hard to know if you're too tense, these signs might give you a hint.

* You start considering setting up an I.V. that will provide you with a steady dose of espresso.
* Relatives who died years ago come visit you and suggest you might want to get some rest.
* You find yourself being chased by trees.
* You and Reality decide to get a divorce.
* Your stock portfolio includes a **lot** of shares in a company that makes antacid and headache tablets.
* You start seeing individual air molecules vibrate.
* You ask yourself if brewing is really essential for the consumption of coffee.

*   You start talking to yourself, and disagree with something you've said. You refuse to speak to yourself for the rest of the day.

* * * * *

I belong to an Internet service that provides inspiring, thought-provoking material. Sometimes it provides hysterical stories too. This true story was sent in by member Pam Butler.

"I was flying from San Francisco to Los Angeles. By the time we took off, there had been a 45-minute delay and everybody on board was ticked.

"Unexpectedly, we stopped in Sacramento on the way. The flight attendant explained that there would be another 45-minute delay, and if we wanted to get off the aircraft, we would re-board in 30 minutes.

"Everybody got off the plane except one gentleman who was blind. I noticed him as I walked by, and could tell he had flown before, because his seeing eye dog had laid quietly underneath the seats in front of him through-out the entire flight. I could also tell he had flown this very flight before because the pilot approached him and, calling him by name, said "Keith, we'll be in Sacramento for almost an hour. Would you like to get off and stretch your legs?" Keith replied, "No thanks, but maybe my dog would like to stretch his."

"Picture this. All the people in the gate area came to a complete standstill when they looked up and saw the pilot walk off the plane with the Seeing Eye dog! The pilot was even wearing sunglasses. People scattered. They not only tried to change planes; they also were trying to change airlines!"

* * * * *

How many times have you gotten offers for a credit card from a company that sends you a letter saying say "pre-approved"? I recently read about a great response. One guy takes the offers he receives, and without providing any of the requested information, puts the application in the postage-paid envelope that's always included with the offers. Then he mails it back. Before he returns it, though, he writes "pre-rejected" on the application.

*   *   *   *   *

Wondering about what your answering-machine message should say? These actual messages might help.

- A is for academics, B is for beer. One of those reasons is why we're not here. So leave a message.
- Hi. This is John. If you are the phone company, I already sent the money. If you are my parents, please send money. If you are my financial aid institution, you didn't lend me enough money. If you are my friend, you owe me money. If you are a female, don't worry, I have plenty of money.
- Hello, this is Sally's microwave. Her answering machine just eloped with her tape deck, so I'm stuck with taking her calls. Say, if you want anything cooked while you leave your message, just hold it up to the phone.
- Hello, you are talking to a machine. I am capable of receiving messages. My owners do not need siding, windows, or a hottub, and their carpets are clean. They give to charity through their office and do not need their picture taken. If you're still with me, leave your name and number and they will get back to you.

- Hi! John's answering machine is broken. This is his refrigerator. Please speak very slowly, and I'll stick your message to myself with one of these magnets.
- Hi. I am probably home. I'm just avoiding someone I don't like. Leave me a message, and if I don't call back, it's you.
- If you are a burglar, then we're probably at home cleaning our weapons right now and can't come to the phone. Otherwise, we probably aren't home and it's safe to leave us a message.
- You're growing tired. Your eyelids are getting heavy. You feel very sleepy now. You are gradually losing your willpower and your ability to resist suggestions. When you hear the tone you will feel helplessly compelled to leave your name, number, and a message.
- Please leave a message. However, you have the right to remain silent. Everything you say will be recorded and used by us.

* * * * *

My wife's wonderful sister Lorraine sent me this hilarious—and true—story:

"I was visiting a sister-in-law one summer afternoon, when my four-year-old niece came running in from outside. My sister-in-law was horrified and embarrassed at her disheveled appearance. The front of the girl's top was a mess.

It was covered with so many stains, it was hard to tell what color the shirt was. I could discern ketchup and mustard from lunch, orange and grape soda, grass and mud stains, and chocolate ice cream, along with other shades which weren't easy to figure out.

"My sister-in-law exclaimed, 'Nicki, what do you have on your shirt!'

"Nicki looked down at her shirt and then back up to her mother. I will never forget the look of joy and pride that beamed from her face when she replied, 'That's my whole day, Mom!"

*   *   *   *   *

Someone much smarter than me (which means it could have been just about anyone) once said "Blessed are they who can laugh at themselves, for they shall never cease to be amused." I definitely agree with that. A while ago, a late-deafened woman who belongs to the same online club as me joked about her poor equilibrium because of an illness. This is a subject I know all too well myself, because my brain tumor has left me with terrible balance. I replied to the woman by joking about my hideous equilibrium, which led to this hilarious response:

"We could have a whole group of different workshops going for us Stagger Pro's. One could be called "Pinball Wizards" and teach people how to ricochet safely from chair to wall. We can also have one called "Confuse a Cop," where we flunk the walk-a-white-line test but pass the breathalizer test with flying colors, leaving the officers scratching their heads in wonder. And we could offer the "John Wayne Workshop," where students learn to stagger and swagger like the big movie star. At the end of that workshop, participants would receive a certificate saying they have the right to sign autographs.

"Just send $19.95 to "Stagger Pro"…money back guarantee (not responsible for bruises)."

*   *   *   *   *

Are you worried that Barbie dolls are only for kids and don't reflect modern life? Well, check out some ideas for new Barbie dolls that would be right for grown-ups.

* **Bifocals Barbie** She comes with her own set of bifocals with six different pairs of fashion frames and half-frames, plus half a dozen editions of *Vogue* and *Vanity Fair*.
* **Hot Flash Barbie** Just press Hot Flash Barbie's bellybutton and her face turns beet red. Tiny drops of sweat appear on her forehead too. Includes a handheld fan and eight dozen tiny tissues.
* **Facial Hair Barbie** Barbie has grown up and her hormone levels have shifted. So now you can see her whiskers grow! Comes with tiny tweezers and a magnifying mirror.
* **Bunion Barbie** Years of disco-dancing in stiletto heels have left Barbie with lots of bunions. Farewell, dainty arched feet! You can soothe her sores with the included pumice stone and plasters, then put the enclosed soft slippers on her.
* **Wrinkles-Be-Gone Barbie** Get rid of those troublesome crow's-feet and lip lines with a tube of *Skin Shine Spackle*, from Barbie's own exclusive line of anti-aging cosmetics.
* **Soccer Mom Barbie** The original Barbie was a cheerleader. Now she's using her old high school megaphone to root for Babs and Ken, Jr. Comes with a tiny mini-van in robin's egg blue and a cooler full of doughnut holes and fruit punch.
* **Mid-life Crisis Barbie** She's ditched Ken and hooked up with Bryce, her personal trainer. She's also started taking Prozac. Barbie's bought a new red Miata, and she and Bryce have moved to Napa Valley and opened a B&B. Includes a tape of "Breaking Up Is Hard To Do."
* **Divorced Barbie** Comes with Ken's house, car, and boat. Ken has shacked up with Barbie and Ken's Swedish *au pair* Ingrid. and

Barbie now lives across town with Babs and Ken, Jr., in a low-rent fourth-floor walk-up. Barbie's selling off her old gowns and accessories to raise rent money.

* **Rehab Barbie** All those parties have taken a real toll on the ultimate party girl. So now she goes to rehab and twelve step meetings instead of stepping out! She's clean and sober, and determined to stay that way.

*   *   *   *   *

In this age of "political correctness" you might want to describe someone who isn't too bright and steer clear of words like "dumb" or "stupid." The following suggestions might help:

* He's a few clowns short of a circus.
* She doesn't have all her dogs on one leash.
* He's all foam and no beer.
* The butter has slipped off her pancake.
* He's almost as smart as bait.
* She's a few fries short of a happy meal.
* He's one fruit loop shy of a full bowl.
* Her antenna doesn't pick up all the channels.
* His belt doesn't go through all the loops.
* She's proof that evolution CAN go in reverse.
* His receiver is off the hook.
* Her skylight isn't overly-bright.
* She has a photographic memory, but the lens cover is still on.
* During evolution his ancestors were in the control group.
* If brains were taxed, she'd get a rebate.

* His gates are down, and his lights are flashing, but the train isn't coming.

* * * * *

Plan to buy a new place? These clarifications of realtor terminology might help.

CHARMING—Can you say "minuscule"? Three of the seven dwarves might fit in it, but the other four and Snow White would definitely have to find a place of their own. Other words that might tip you off to a size-impaired place include "Cute," "Enchanting," and "Good Starter Home."

MUCH POTENTIAL—A potential disaster. You definitely don't want to buy a place like this unless your need to spend money is great.

UNIQUE CITY HOME—If houses could speak, this one would say "I used to be a warehouse."

DARING DESIGN—**Still** a warehouse.

ONE-OF-A-KIND—A polite way of saying "ugly as sin."

MUST SEE TO BELIEVE—You definitely don't want to believe.

BRILLIANT CONCEPT—Has a two-story live oak in its 30-foot sky dome.

YOU'LL LOVE IT—If you're an android.

* * * * *

Mark, who's an avid reader, went to a bookstore and asked the saleswoman "Where's the self-help section?" She said if she told him it would defeat the purpose.

* * * * *

I'm seriously addicted to writing, and know that doing it well means learning its ins and outs. Here are a few suggestions.

* Always avoid alliteration.
* Never use a long word when a diminutive one will do.
* Avoid ampersands & abbreviations, etc.
* Steer clear of parenthetical remarks (however relevant).
* Be sure to never split an infinitive.
* There's no need for contractions.
* Foreign words and phrases are not *apropos*.
* You should always avoid quotations. As Ralph Waldo Emerson said, "I hate quotations. Tell me what you know."
* Don't be redundant or repetitive.
* Ever want to use a one-word sentence? Don't.
* The passive voice should never be employed.
* Avoid colloquialisms and cliches like the plague.

* * * * *

Speaking of writing, many journalists learn early on that there are five 'w's and one 'h' in good article writing: "who," "what," "where," "when," "why," and "how." They're an important part of any journalist's approach. I had to laugh, though, when I read that a college journalism student, in answer to a test question, identified them as "writing," "wondering," "working," "worrying," "who knows?" and "HELP!"

* * * * *

In the chapter about hearing, I shared a hilarious (and true) story about a carpet-cleaning company telemarketer who called a late-deafened man. If you want to get rid of a telemarketer, you might try one of these approaches.

* If a telemarketer wants to lend you some money, tell him or her you just filed for bankruptcy and you could definitely use some dough. Ask how long you can keep it, if you ever have to pay it back, or if it's like the other money you borrowed before your bankruptcy.

* Your telemarketer might start with something like "How are you today?" If that happens, say "Why do you want to know?" Then go into how your heart murmur is acting up, your eyelashes are sore, and your dog just died.

* The telemarketer will probably tell you something like his name is Rufus Doofus from the Acme Company. Respond by asking him to spell his and the firm's name, then ask where the company is located. Keep asking the telemarketer questions about himself and the company until he hangs up.

* After the telemarketer identifies him/herself, adopt a tone of utter joy and cry out whatever the telemarketer's first name is. Then say "It's so good to hear from you. I can't believe it! How have you been?" With any luck, this will give the telemarketer a few brief moments of sheer terror as s/he tries to figure out where s/he could know you from.

* When the telemarketer tries to make the sale, say "No," over and over. Be creative about it too—vary the sound and pitch of each "no," Don't let the telemarketer get a word in. Keep it up until s/he hangs up.

* A lot of long-distance companies offer programs called "Family and Friends" or somesuch. If one of them calls and tries to sell

you their plan, adopt a totally sinister voice and say, "I don't have any friends…would you be my friend?"

* Let the telemarketer go through his/her spiel, and provide feedback in the form of an occasional "Uh-huh" or "That's fascinating." After a little while, the telemarketer will ask you to buy the product or service s/he's pitching. That's when you ask him/her to marry you. That's sure to make the telemarketer seriously flustered. When s/he questions that, say you couldn't possibly give your credit card number to a total stranger.

* * * * *

Here are some actual signs seen at various residences, businesses, and en-tertainment facilities that will make you think twice about visiting, shopping, or watching something there.

* Elephants please stay in your car.
* The farmer allows walkers to cross the field for free, but the bull charges.
* If you cannot read, this leaflet will tell you how to get lessons.
* We can repair anything. (Please knock hard on the door—the bell doesn't work)
* Beware! I shoot every tenth trespasser and the ninth one has just left.

* * * * *

Americans do lots of traveling for both work and pleasure, and some of the interactions they've had with travel agents are absolutely staggering. Here are just a few of the funnier (and real) ones.

* A woman called her travel agent and said she wanted to go to Capetown. The agent started explaining the length of the flight and the passport information she'd need to provide. The caller interrupted the agent by saying, "I'm not trying to make you look stupid, but Capetown is in Massachusetts." The agent didn't want to make the caller feel stupid either, so she calmly explained, "Cape Cod is in Massachusetts, Capetown is in South Africa." The caller's response? Click.

* A man called a travel agency, and expressed his anger about a Florida package the agency did. The agent asked what was wrong with the vacation. The caller said he was expecting an ocean-view room in Orlando. The agent explained that wasn't possible, since Orlando is in the middle of the state. The caller replied with "Don't lie to me. I looked on the map, and Florida is a very thin state."

* Another geographically-impaired traveler asked his travel agent if it was possible to see England from Canada. When the agent answered with a "No," the caller said "But they look so close on the map."

* A woman called her travel agent and asked how it was possible that her flight from Detroit left at 8:20 am and arrived in Chicago at 8:33 am. The agent tried to explain that time in Michigan was an hour ahead of that in Illinois, but the caller couldn't understand the concept of time zones. So the agent finally told her that the plane went very fast. The caller bought that.

* A customer called and said, "I need to fly to Pepsi-Cola on one of those computer planes." The agent asked the caller if she meant she wanted to fly to Pensacola on a commuter plane. The caller said, "Yeah, whatever."

* A businessman called and asked a question about the documents he'd need in order to fly to China. The agent told the man he'd need a visa. "Oh no I don't," he replied, "I've been to China four times and every time they have accepted my American Express."

Tea Time

◆

Clothing generally isn't very funny—except for t-shirts! Here are some of the best I've ever seen. I hope you'll find one that "fits" you.

* * * * *

- * (Around a picture of dandelions) I Fought the Lawn and the Lawn Won
- * Microbiology Laboratory: Staph Only
- * I Suffer Occasional Delusions of Adequacy
- * At My Age, I've Seen it All, Done it All, Heard it All…I Just Can't Remember it All
- * I Just Do What the Voices Inside My Head Tell Me to Do
- * (For pregnant women) A Man Did This to Me, Oprah
- * Princess, Having Had Sufficient Experience with Princes, Seeks Frog
- * (On the back of a passing motorcyclist's T-shirt) If You Can Read This, My Wife Fell Off
- * I Used to be Schizophrenic, But We're OK Now
- * Veni, Vedi, Visa: I Came, I Saw, I Did a Little Shopping

- (On the Front) Yale is Just One Big Party (On the back) With a $25,000 Cover Charge
- Liberal Arts Major…Will Think for Money
- IRS—Be Audit You Can Be
- Gravity…It's Not Just a Good Idea. It's the Law.
- If They Don't Have Chocolate in Heaven, I Ain't Going
- My Mother is a Travel Agent for Guilt Trips
- (Seen at a Gay Pride parade) My Son Just Came Out of the Closet and All I Got Was This Lousy T-Shirt
- First National Bank of Dad—Sorry, Closed
- (Seen at Cape Cod) If it's Called "Tourist Season," Why Can't We Hunt Them?
- Love May be Blind, But Marriage is a Real Eye-Opener
- If at First You Don't Succeed, Skydiving isn't For You
- Get a New Car For Your Spouse; It'll Be a Great Trade
- Dinner Is Ready When the Smoke Alarm Goes Off
- Old Age Comes At a Bad Time
- In My Next Life I'm Going To Have More Memory Installed
- Love Your Enemies; It'll Drive 'em Crazy
- People Who Think They Know Everything are Very Annoying to Those of Us Who Do
- Why be Difficult When With a Bit of Effort You Can be Impossible?
- Work Fascinates Me: I Could Sit and Watch It for Hours
- (On a picture of a computer screen) You Have Performed an Illegal Operation and Your Existence Must be Terminated
- You're Only Young Once…But You Can be Immature Forever!

- I Yell Because I Care
- In Dog Years…I'm Dead
- Your Village Called…They Want Their Idiot Back!
- Dear Lord; If You Can't Make Me Skinny Please Make My Friends Fat
- My Kids Did This To Me
- I Pretend to Work…They Pretend to Pay Me
- I'm Multi-Talented—I Can Talk and Piss You Off at the Same Time
- Old Enough to Know Better…Young Enough to Do It Anyway!
- Consciousness: That Annoying Time Between Naps
- Dropt On My Hed When I Wuz a Kid
- So Many Idiots…So Few Comets
- (Above a picture of Mt. Rushmore) In Concert—America's Greatest Rock Group
- (Around a picture of the Earth as seen from the moon) Visualize Whirled Peas
- I Work for Peanuts—I Should be Working for Chocolate
- Cleverly Disguised as a Responsible Adult
- What If the Hokey-Pokey is Really What it's All About?
- Be Nice To Your Kids: They'll Choose Your Nursing Home
- (On a picture of a computer floppy disc) The Name is Baud. James Baud.
- (Also on a picture of a computer floppy disc) Bad Command or File Name: Go Stand in Corner
- (On a picture of a computer screen) Access Denied…. Nah, Nah, Nah, Nah, Nah!

* (Under a picture of William Shakespeare) Bard to the Bone
* (Also under a picture of "Willy the Hook") Have a Nice Play
* A Day Without Sunshine is Like Night
* (Beneath a picture of animals in a classroom, taking an exam) Against Animal Testing
* Hand Over the Chocolate and No One Gets Hurt!
* (Beneath a picture of three cavemen carrying a huge carrot) Early Vegetarians Returning From the Kill
* Alcohol & Calculus Don't Mix: Never Drink and Derive
* (On a picture of a floppy disk) File Not Found. Should I Fake It?
* Clones are People Two
* I Don't Suffer from Insanity—I Enjoy Every Minute of It
* I Think—Therefore I Can't Sleep
* I Want to be My Own Boss, But My Wife Won't Let Me
* I'm No Lady: I'm a Lawyer!
* If a Cow Laughed Would Milk Come Out Her Nose?
* If You're Born Again, Do You Have Two Bellybuttons?
* It's Not an Empty Nest Until They Get Their Stuff Out of the Basement
* Old Age Is No Place for Sissies
* Picked Last in Gym
* (On a picture of a computer floppy disc) Smash Forehead on Keyboard to Continue
* Taxation **With** Representation Isn't So Hot Either
* You! Out of the Gene Pool!
* (On a picture of a newspaper, the headline of which reads) The 21st Century: History is Finally Old Enough to Drink

* THNIK
* (Under a picture of a brain) Warning: Fragile Ego System!
* Why is the Alphabet in that Order—is it Because of That Song?
* Jesus Saves, Passes to Moses, He Shoots, Scores!
* If You Can Read This You're Violating My Personal Space
* I is a College Student
* If a Man Speaks in a Forest, and There is No Woman There to Hear Him, is He Still Wrong?
* I Love my Grandchildren; I Should Have Had Them First.
* My Wife Says I Don't Listen to Her—At Least That's What I Think She Said
* Born in the USA…a Long, Long, Time Ago
* I Didn't Escape; They Gave Me a Daypass
* A Man Chases a Woman Until She Catches Him
* (On a picture of a floppy disc) Bad Command > Bad, Bad Command. Sit! Stay!
* (Also on a picture of a floppy disc) Does Fuzzy Logic Tickle?
* (On still another picture of a floppy disc) Southern DOS: Ya'll Reckon? _ (Yep/Nope)
* Be More or Less Specific
* Earthling
* Few Women Admit Their Age. Few Men Act It.
* Free the Elves!
* Gambling with our Kid's Inheritance
* Golf is a Game Where You Yell "Fore," Shoot Six, and Write Down "Five"
* My Moon Must be in Stupid

- (Around the letters "M" and "D" and a picture of the M.D. symbol) Massive Debt
- Slackers Unite—Tomorrow!
- Some Day We'll Look Back on This and Plow Into a Parked Car
- Super Callused Fragile Mystic Plagued With Halitosis
- To be worn by kids:
  - —$500 Tax Credit
  - —If I Don't Get It From Santa, there's Always Grandma and Grandpa
  - —Raised by Wolves
  - —Patent Pending
  - —My Parents Got Me At a Fleamarket
  - —Boys are Weird & They Have Cooties
  - —Organically Grown
  - —Show Me the Presents
- The Face is Familiar: But I Can't Remember My Name
- Too Many Freaks, Not Enough Comets
- (On a picture of a floppy disk) Upgrades: Take Old Bugs Out, Put New Bugs In
- (Also on a picture of a floppy disk) Who is General Failure and Why is He Reading my Disk?
- C:/DOS, C:/DOS/RUN, RUN/DOS/RUN
- (Around a picture of a nasty-looking dog wearing sunglasses) Bad Dog (baad dawg) n 1. Has No Master 2. Knows Attitude Is Everything 3. Absolutely NO Leashes!
- (Next to a picture of a warning sign) Smash Head on Keyboard to Continue
- Ladies Sewing Circle and Terrorist Society

- (Over a picture of a cat sleeping) I Don't Do Mornings
- (Under a picture of a pooch eating a hot dog) Dog Eat Dog
- I Almost Had a Psychic Girlfriend, but She Left Me Before We Met
- I Survived Catholic School
- A Women's Place is in the House—and Senate
- I Have Abandoned my Search for Reality, and am Now Looking for a Good Fantasy
- I'm Not Pregnant; I'm a Watermelon Thief
- When God Made Men, She was Only Joking
- If You Talk to God, You're Praying. If God Talks to You, You Have Schizophrenia.
- (On a picture of a door-hanger) Already Disturbed
- (Under a picture of a dog and cat on thrones) Reigning Cats and Dogs
- There's Nothing Wrong With Me That a Humongous Scoop of Chocolate Ice Cream Can't Cure.
- I Have Too Seen Elvis!
- I am Woman; I'm Invincible; I'm Dead Tired
- My Rod and my Reel; They Comfort Me
- My Parents were Abducted by Aliens and All They Brought Me was This Lousy T-shirt
- Make My Golf Ball Rest in Green Pastures, Not in Still Waters
- (Around a picture of a putting green) I'm Not Over the Hill; I'm Just On the Back Nine
- On Advice of My Attorney, My T-shirt Has No Comment
- I'm Not Opinionated. I'm Just Always Right.

* If Life is a Stage, I Need a Stronger Spotlight
* Kick Me!
* Not Only am I Perfect, I'm a Grandmother Too
* Doesn't Play Well With Others
* (Around the number 50) Young at Heart: Other Parts Slightly Older
* If It's Not One Thing, It's Your Mother
* M(ust) O(bey) M(e)
* Being a Woman Isn't Easy…It Requires Dealing With Men
* (Around a picture of jail-cell bars) My Child was Inmate of the Month at County Jail
* One Tequila, Two Tequila, Three Tequila, Floor.
* Lord grant me the serenity to accept the things I cannot change, the courage to change the things I can, and the wisdom to hide the bodies of those people I had to kill because they pissed me off!
* I'm a Relic of the 60's
* My Good Clothes are in the Wash
* Multi-tasking: Screwing Up Several Things At Once
* (Above a picture of a man sleeping at a desk) I'm Not Unemployed; I'm a Consultant
* (Also above a picture of a man sleeping at a desk) I Love My Job; It's the Work I Hate
* (Around a picture of a man at a computer) Technology: Not For the Faint of Heart
* Question Reality
* I'm Not Bald; I'm Just Taller Than My Hair

- Old Age: No Place for Wimps
- Ladies Sewing Circle and Terrorist Society
- (Over a picture of a cat lying on the floor) I Don't Do Mornings
- (Under a picture of a pooch eating a frankfurter) Dog Eat Dog
- I'm Roadkill On the Information Superhighway
- (Under a picture of dinosaurs smoking) The Real Reason Dinosaurs Became Extinct
- Danger: Men Cooking
- If I Want to Hear the Pitter-Patter of Little Feet, I'll Put Shoes On My Cat
- At Home, I'm the Boss—After My Wife
- Coffee, Chocolate, Men…Some Things are Just Better Rich
- (Above a picture of a baby) Man of the House
- (Under a picture of two weevils, with an arrow pointing to the shorter one) Lesser of Two Weevils
- Who are Those Kids, and Why are They Calling Me "Mom?"
- I'm Not Getting Older…I'm Getting Bitter
- (Under a picture of a computer keyboard) All Wight. Rho Svitched My Keytops Around?
- (On a picture of a floppy disk) Congress sys corrupted. Reboot Washington, D.C.? _ Yes _ No
- (On a picture of a movie rating) IA: For Immature Audiences Only
- Morally Impaired
- Tree Hugger
- There's Definitely Something Wrong With Me
- God Made Us Sisters; Prozac Made Us Friends

* If You Want Breakfast in Bed, Sleep in the Kitchen
* Next Mood Swing: Six Minutes
* Save Energy: Sleep in Class
* The Older I Get, the Better I Was
* My Mind Works Like Lightning—One Brilliant Flash and It's Gone!
* I am a Bomb Technician; If You See Me Running You Should Keep Up
* For Every Action, There is an Equal and Opposite Government Program
* Give a Man a Fish and He'll Eat for a Day; Teach a Man to Fish and He'll Sit Around and Drink Beer All Day
* Money isn't Everything, But It Keeps the Kids in Touch
* Formula for Success:1) Work Hard 2) Dress Right 3) Win the Lottery
* Nobody Knows I'm Elvis
* I'm Not Short; I'm Altitudinally Challenged
* Warning: Retiree; Knows It All and Has Plenty of Time to Tell You About It!
* If Stress Burned Calories, I'd Be a Size 5
* You Have the Right To Remain Silent; Anything You Say Will Be Misquoted, Then Used Against You
* I Wish the Buck Stopped Here; I Could Use a Few
* This Body is a Temple: Chocolate Worshipped Daily
* The Problem with Opportunity is that it Only Knocks. Temptation Kicks in the Door
* I'd Quit This Job, But I Need the Sleep

* I Have the Body of a God; Unfortunately, It's Buddha
* I Miss My Ex, But My Aim is Improving
* Ex-wife for Sale; Just Take Over Payments
* If You Can Read This Pull Me Back in the Boat
* Cinderella was Thrown Off the Basketball Team Because She Ran Away from the Ball
* Out of Estrogen and I've Got a Gun!

The Technodunce

◆

Not long after I lost my hearing in 1991 and joined the Association of Late-Deafened Adults, the group's co-founder jokingly referred to himself as "Bill 'Techno-dunce' Graham." I laughed really hard when I read that. But I knew the truth—**I'm** the real technodunce. A case in point: my wife and I have an iMac, which is one of the most forgiving computers ever invented, but I still manage to make techno-boo-boo's with it all the time. And the book **Macs for Dummies** was way too advanced for me. If you need physical evidence, you should know that when the talk turns to technology, I break out in a cold sweat.

I've also learned, though, that technology can be the source of some of the funniest material around. So take a "byte" of the following.

*   *   *   *   *

You might feel bad because you underestimated the importance of computers and data processing in the modern world. Well, don't sweat it. Some of the "great minds" in the technology world did too, as these comments prove.

"I think there is a world market for maybe five computers."

—Thomas Watson, chairman of IBM, 1943

"Computers in the future may weigh no more than 1.5 tons."

—*Popular Mechanics*, writing about the "down-sizing" of computers, 1949

"I have traveled the length and breadth of this country and talked with the best people, and I can assure you that data processing is a fad that won't last out the year."

—The business books editor for Prentice Hall, 1957

"But what…is it good for?"

—An engineer in the Advanced Computing Systems Division of IBM, commenting on the microchip, 1968.

"There is no reason anyone would want a computer in their home."

—Ken Olson, president, chairman, and founder of Digital Equipment Corp., 1977

"640K ought to be enough for anybody."

—Bill Gates (Microsoft's main man), 1981

*   *   *   *   *

Unless you've been in hibernation for several years, you know that viruses can cause real problems for computer users. They're all frightening (the viruses, not the computer users!), and I recently heard about one that's truly scary. It's called "the work virus."

How do you get "the work virus?" There are two ways: via e-mail or by unwittingly downloading it from the Internet. Any file with the word "work" in it may carry the virus, and should be deleted as soon as possible. If you don't do that, and your computer is infected, you'll send an e-mail to your boss that says "This job is such a waste of my brain power. I think I'll go to the closest gin joint."

Then you'll do it. You'll grab no fewer than three friends, don a hat and coat, and head for your favorite local bar. You'll then order at least four pitchers of beer or two dozen hard drinks—or both! You'll drink all of them, forget all about work, and find yourself in a spirited conversation about how the comics page of your local paper has changed your life.

In the interest of helping others keep their job, please e-mail this message to all your friends. If you don't have any friends, or you have no social life, the dreaded "work" virus may have already victimized you. You have my sympathy....

*   *   *   *   *

Speaking of viruses, computer users should watch out for another one that's particularly scary:"The Strunkenwhite Virus," named to honor the authors of a book every writer knows about—**The Elements of Style** by William Strunk, Jr. and E. B. White.

How does "The Strunkenwhite Virus" work? Simple. It returns all e-mail messages that have grammatical errors in them. Unlike the spell-checkers that now come with word-processing programs, The Strunkenwhite Virus finds any and all style errors in writing, and is particularly unforgiving.

Corporate America has become thoroughly accustomed to the missing words and pained syntax so common in cyberspace. But The Strunkenwhite Virus doesn't allow any of that. It will seize any e-mail that misuses the English language and return it to the creator. A nameless corporate executive recently said with great sadness: "Whenever I tried to send an e-mail this morning, it came bouncing back to me with this error message: 'A participial phrase at the beginning of a sentence must refer to the grammatical subject.' I got so depressed I threw my laptop out the window."

There's been lots of speculation as to who created the virus. One broker suggested the creator is a disgruntled English major who couldn't make it on the trading floor. Other business honchos have expressed fear that The Strunkenwhite Virus could make e-mailing unlikely, because office workers unsure of their writing skill might be afraid to send legitimate computer correspondence to current or potential clients. On the good side, though, workers might be afraid to use company time to play on the Internet, or trade e-mail jokes or trivia with their spouses, parents, and friends for fear of receiving or spreading the virus.

The Strunkenwhite Virus has caused particular chaos in government e-mail. Several government agencies are unable to use e-mail now because they violate one of the virus's central rules: "Do not overwrite." The virus also dictates: "Be clear." Those of you who have had the misfortune of reading government writing know these guidelines are virtually impossible for most bureaucrats to follow.

The virus has also affected several home computer users. The virus catches any use of "breezy" language and says computer-users "must not inject opinion" into their files and e-mails.

Meanwhile, bookstores report that orders for **The Elements of Style** have surged incredibly.

* * * * *

Speaking of viruses, here are a few others you should be on the lookout for.

* ADAM AND EVE Virus: Bytes your Apple.
* AIRLINE Virus: You've flown to Miami, but your data is in Los Angeles.
* CONGRESSIONAL Virus: Your computer locks up, and the screen divides almost equally, with a message appearing on each half blaming the other side for whatever problem that's current.
* DAN QUAYLE Virus: Forces your computer to play PGA TOUR from 10 am to 4 pm, six days a week and adds e's to the end of all vegetable words (i.e. "potato" becomes "potatoe," and so on).
* ELVIS Virus: Your computer gains weight and self-destructs. Clones then appear in bars, shopping malls, and casinos all across America.
* FEDERAL BUREAUCRAT Virus: Does virtually nothing, but claims to be the most important part of your computer.
* FREUDIAN Virus: Makes your computer want to marry its own motherboard.
* GALLUP Virus: 54 percent of all PCs infected with this virus will lose 42 percent of their data 17 percent of the time (plus or minus 3.5 percent).
* HMO Virus: Tests your system for no more than an hour, finds nothing wrong with it, and says your insurance doesn't cover computer viruses.
* MARTHA STEWART Virus: Redesigns your desktop in tasteful, muted pastels.
* TABLOID Virus: Constantly scans your files for evidence that you're secretly related to aliens, or are planning to take over the planet with Marilyn Monroe

* OLLIE NORTH Virus: Turns your computer into a paper shredder.
* PAT BUCHANAN Virus: Turns your keyboard sharply to the right.
* PAUL REVERE Virus: There's no horsing around with this virus—it warns you of impending hard disk attacks—once if by LAN, twice if by C.
* PBS Virus: Your computer asks you for money every few minutes.
* POLITICALLY CORRECT Virus: This bug identifies itself as an "electronic micro-organism."
* RICHARD NIXON or TRICKY DICK Virus: Repeats the phrase "I'm not a crook" over and over. You might be able to wipe it out, but it always comes back.
* ROSS PEROT Virus: Displays a message every time you start up your computer saying it's thinking of running. It then scans your hard disk for competing operating systems, and closes down immediately if it finds any other viruses.
* SEARS Virus: Harmless unless you fail to buy a huge television, a new wardrobe, and 800 bags of fertilizer.
* TED KENNEDY Virus: Infects your computer, then swears it never happened.
* TED TURNER Virus: Colorizes your black-and-white printer.
* TEXAS Virus: The biggest virus of all—and darn proud of that!
* TYPE-A Virus: Ensures your hard drive is hard-driven.
* U.N. Virus: Takes complete control of all of your computer's defensive and offensive programs. It isn't answerable to anyone or anything, but can't accomplish anything.

* * * * *

At a recent computer expo, Microsoft big-wheel Bill Gates reportedly compared the computer industry to the auto industry and said that if General Motors "had kept up with technology like the computer world has, we'd all be driving $25 cars that got 1000 miles to the gallon." GM later issued a statement asking if consumers would really want a car that crashed twice a day. After I stopped laughing at the GM response, I started wondering if these things would happen if Microsoft made cars.

* Would drivers be constantly pressured to upgrade their cars?
* Would all cars run only on Microsoft gas?
* Would car warning lights for the oil, alternator, gas, and engine be replaced by a 'GENERAL CAR FAULT' warning light?
* Would only one person be allowed in a car at any time, unless owners bought CarNT or the latest version of "Car—"?
* Would the car die for no apparent reason on a regular basis? And would drivers simply consider this normal?
* Would we have buy a new car every time the lines on the road were repainted?

   * * * * *

Similarly, if Microsoft moved to Georgia, you might encounter these changes.

* "Microsoft Windows" would become "Microsoft Winders."
* Its popular "Powerpoint" program would be renamed "ParPawnt."
* "ParPawnt" would be re-designed to have "Pond Scum" and "Junk Yard" presentation templates.
* The hourglass icon would be replaced with a picture of an emptying beer bottle.

* Opening certain files would bring up a window that was covered with a plastic garbage bag and duct tape.
* "Yes," "No," and "Cancel," dialogue boxes would be replaced with these options: "Aww-right," "Naw," and "Git."
* Activating a Microsoft application wouldn't produce the familiar "Ta-Dah!" sound. Instead you'd get "Dueling Banjos."
* Microsoft VP's would be called "Cuz."
* Microsoft main-man Bill Gates would be re-named "Billy-Bob" or "Bubba" Gates.
* A new screen saver would say "This computer protected by Smith and Wesson."
* The spell checker on Microsoft Word would be phonetic, and offer spellings like this: "Hookt on fonics werkt 4 me."

* * * * *

Ever wondered if you're an Internet geek? These geekdom-guidelines might help you find out.

* You used to make conversation with a prospective date by asking what his/her sign was. Now you say "What's your URL?"
* You're filling out an application and where it says "address" you give your e-mail address.
* Your spouse no longer calls you to dinner: s/he sends you an email.
* You're amazed to learn that "Spam" is a food.
* You introduce your wife or husband as "spouse@home.com."
* Instead of kissing your girlfriend, you kiss her home page.

* You won't take a vacation to any place that doesn't have electricity and phone lines.
* You break down and take a vacation, but spend half of the plane trip with your child in the overhead compartment and your laptop computer on your lap.
* Your daydreams used to be about fame, wealth, and happiness, but now they're about getting a faster connection to the Internet.
* When you turn off your modem you get this awful, empty feeling, like you just pulled the plug on the life-support system of a loved one.
* You start introducing yourself as "Joe8 at AOL dot com."
* Contact with your mother becomes history because she doesn't have a modem.
* All of your friends have an @ in their names.
* Your dog and cat have their own home pages.
* **And scariest of all:** You name your children Eudora, Search, and Dotcom.

* * * * *

Sending your computer in for repair can cost a small fortune. So I recommend the following do-it-yourself approach.
* Grab the mouse thingy.
* Click on the whatyacallit.
* Scroll down to the third thingamagig.
* Highlight the third thingamagig and copy it. Then paste it to the whatchamacallit.

* After you do that, go to the gizmo.
* Re-install the whozit in the gadget.
* Put the boots back on your computer.

Works for me every time!

    *   *   *   *   *

Do computers have a gender? And if they do, are they men or women?

My friend Brenda is convinced they're male. Why? Because they're so much like male humanoids. Here are just a few of her reasons:

* Computers and men both have lots of data but are still totally clueless.
* A better model is always just around the corner.
* Both look nice and shiny until you bring them home.
* They'll do whatever you say if you push the right buttons.
* Playing games with either one is great fun.

Ed doesn't see it that way, though. He's convinced computers are women. Why?

* No one but their creator understands the internal logic of computers.
* The smallest mistakes computer users make are immediately committed to memory for future reference.
* The native language computers use is incomprehensible.
* Computers often give messages like: "Bad command or file name." Confusing and frustrating to be sure, just like when a

woman says something like "If you don't know why I'm mad at you, then I'm certainly not going to tell you."

* If you buy a computer, you'll spend half your paycheck on accessories for it.

  *   *   *   *   *

Computer users often call customer support and ask some truly amazing questions. Here are just a few of the stranger—and real—calls I've read about.

* An exasperated woman called a help-line and said she could't get her new computer to turn on. The technician made sure the computer was plugged in and then asked the woman what happened when she pushed the power button. "I've pushed and pushed on this foot pedal and nothing happens," she replied. The confused technician asked."Foot pedal?" "Yes," the woman replied, "this little white foot pedal with the on switch." It turned out that the "foot pedal," was the computer's mouse.

* One computer company's help center recently got a call from a frustrated customer who said her new computer wouldn't work. She said she had unpacked the unit, plugged it in, opened it up, and then sat there for 20 minutes waiting for something to happen. And nothing did. The technical support person asked the caller what happened when she pressed the power switch. The woman's reply? "What power switch?"

* Some new computer users are just plain baffled by the language their machines use. A technical support employee reports that several "new-bies" have called to ask where the "any" key is after seeing the words "Press Any Key" flash on their screen.

- Other people have had trouble figuring out the mouse on their computer. One customer called technical support and complained that her mouse was hard to control with the "dust cover" on it. The "dust cover" was actually the plastic bag the mouse was packaged in.
- Another customer was told by a tech support person to send in a copy of a defective floppy disk. A letter from the customer arrived a few days later, along with a photocopy of a floppy disk.
- One technician told his customer to put his floppy back in the computer's disk drive and "close the door." The customer agreed, and told the technician "hold on." The customer put the phone down and the technician heard him shut the door to his room.
- Another caller complained that his keyboard no longer worked. He had cleaned it, he said, and couldn't figure out the problem. How did he clean the keyboard? By filling up his tub with soap and water, soaking the keyboard for a day, and then removing all the keys from it and washing them individually.

* * * * *

In the chapter about animals, I talked about how certain well-known individuals might have answered the age-old question "Why did the chicken cross the road?" Would the computer world have answered like this?

- The chicken will cross the road in June. No, August. October for sure.
- The Microsoft Chicken (TM) is already on both sides of the road. In fact, it just bought the road.

* Chickens don't need to cross the road anymore. They can just send an e-mail.
* If it's a Java Chicken, and the road needs to be crossed, the server will simply download a chicken to the other side.
* COBOL Chicken: 0001-CHICKEN-CROSSING. IF NO-MORE-VEHICLES, PERFORM 0010-CROSS-THE-ROAD VARYING STEPS FROM 1 BY 1 UNTIL ON-THE-OTHER-SIDE.
* The Macinchicken cannot cross PC roads without special feathers.

Take My WordPlay For It

♦

I confess! I **love** any kind of humor based on how we use (and abuse!) language. So in the pages that follow, you'll run into more wordplay than you've probably ever seen before. It may leave you laughing or groaning (in joy, misery, or both). Whatever happens, though, I hope it will take you on a health-inducing "internal jog."

* * * * *

Did you hear about the bear who went over the mountain to see what was bruin?

* * * * *

How about those guys who were paddling around a lake and were really cold. They lit a small fire in their kayak, which spread lickety-split. The boat sank, which I guess proves that you can't have your kayak and heat it too.

* * * * *

Rick plays a lot of chess, and a while ago he went to a convention about the game. The conventioneers were standing around in the hotel lobby one evening and talking about—no surprise here, really—how they'd become so good at the game and the honors their chess skill had brought them. The manager of the hotel came by and broke into song:"Chess Nuts Boasting In an Open Foyer."

*   *   *   *   *

A student was reading a book about the history of Europe, and learned that the guy who threw a grenade into a French kitchen was named "Linoleum Blownapart."

*   *   *   *   *

Jim was heavily into all sorts of New Age things, including transcendental meditation. When he went to get a filling recently, the dentist prepared to give him some local anesthetic before he started the work. But Jim said "no" because he wanted to transcend dental medication.

*   *   *   *   *

Want to justify your love for word-play? The business world has found that clever wording can be a real money-maker. Here a few signs that appeared inside and near various businesses, or on their trucks and vans.

- *   Next to a motel: "Come in and take a road off your mind"
- *   In an antique shop: "Den of antiquity"
- *   Over another antique shop: "Remains to be seen"
- *   At a tire store: "We skid you not"

- Another tire store's sign said: "Time to re-tire"
- In a health club: "Only 27 shaping days 'til Christmas"
- Inside a reducing salon: "A word to the wide is sufficient"
- In the window of a watch-repair store: "If it doesn't tick, talk to us"
- In a Podiatrist's office: "Time wounds all heels"
- A garden shop sign said: "We will sell no vine before its time"
- In a body shop: "May we have the next dents?"
- At a dentist's office: "Always be true to your teeth or they will be false to you"
- Over a watch display in a jewelry store: "There's no present like the time"
- In a veterinarian's waiting room: "Be back in 5 minutes. Sit! Stay!"
- On a butcher's window: "Let me meat your needs"
- On the door of a computer store: "Out for a quick byte"
- On an electric company van: "Power to the people"
- In an ice cream and dairy store: "You can't beat our milkshakes, but you can whip our cream and lick our ice cream cones"
- Outside a Hotel: "Help! We need inn-experienced people"
- At an optometrist's office: "If you don't see what you're looking for, you've come to the right place"
- In a restaurant window: "Don't stand there and be hungry, come on in and get fed up"

*   *   *   *   *

Anagrams

As you probably learned way back when, an anagram is a word or phrase you create by rearranging the letters of another word or phrase. We're not always talking about a single word or two either. Here's a truly amazing anagram from Shakespeare's masterful play **Hamlet**. The original, which many of us know, says: "To be or not to be, that is the question, whether 'tis nobler in the mind to suffer the slings and arrows of outrageous fortune…" A little playing around, though, yields this truly amazing anagram: "In one of the Bard's best-thought-of tragedies, our insistent hero, Hamlet, queries on two fronts about how life turns rotten."

There's more too. When he became the first Earthling to walk on the moon, Neil Armstrong said "That's one small step for a man, one giant leap for mankind." If you re-arrange the letters, though, you get: "Thin man ran, makes a large stride, left planet, pins flag on moon. On to Mars!"

Here are a few shorter anagrams.

The Original	The Anagram
Woody Allen	A lewd loony
William Shakespeare	I am a weakish speller
Sir Arthur Canon Doyle	Horrendous carnality
Gore's letters	Less to regret
George Bush	He bugs Gore
Margaret Thatcher	That great charmer
The Conservative Party	Teacher in vast poverty
Dormitory	Dirty room
Slot Machines	Cash lost in 'em
Animosity	Is no amity

Mother-in-law	Woman Hitler
Alec Guinness	Genuine class
Semolina	Is no meal
The Public Art Galleries	Large picture halls, I bet
A Decimal Point	I'm a dot in place
The Earthquakes	That queer shake
Eleven Plus Two	Twelve plus one
Contradiction	Accord not in it
The Morse Code	Here come dots
Snooze Alarms	Alas! No more z's
Princess Diana	Ascend in Paris
Astronomer	Moon starer

* * * * *

You've probably run across more than a few mixed metaphors, which join two very different ideas or descriptions. Politicians are particularly prone to them, but the following (which are all real), are truly hysterical, regardless of their source.

- * I wouldn't be caught dead in that movie with a ten-foot pole.
- * The sacred cows have come home to roost with a vengeance.
- * Milwaukee is the golden egg that the rest of the state wants to milk.
- * That's a very hard blow to swallow.
- * It's time to swallow the bullet.
- * That snake in the grass is barking up the wrong tree.

* When we get to that bridge, we'll jump.
* Don't sit there like a sore thumb.
* It's time to grab the bull by the tail and look it in the eye.

* * * * *

Did you hear about the florist who thought his son was a budding genius? Unfortunately, the boy turned out to be a blooming idiot.

* * * * *

Then there was the police officer who accidentally arrested a supreme court official who was dressed up as a notorious criminal for a costume party. Tsk, tsk: you should never book a judge by his cover.

* * * * *

Did you hear about the man who went out fishing? He dropped his wallet overboard. He thought the wallet was gone forever, but two carps appeared right away, and held the wallet at the surface by bouncing it back and forth between them. You could call it "Carp-to-Carp-Walleting."

* * * * *

I wonder.... Lawyers can be disbarred and clergymen defrocked. Can electricians be delighted, musicians denoted, cowboys deranged, models deposed, or dry cleaners depressed?

* * * * *

A rancher needed a new bull. So he went to a livestock auction with his workers and got one, which he promptly named "Caesar." On the walk home, the farmer and his workers came to a river they'd crossed on their way to the auction. The farmer went off to look at different parts of the river and boats he could rent to transport the bull across it.

The workers wanted to do a little swimming before getting on the boat to cross, so they went to the banks of the river. The bull, meanwhile, munched on some grass. A few minutes later, the farmer returned and saw what was happening. He was furious, and shouted at the workers "We came to ferry Caesar, not to graze him!"

*   *   *   *   *

A patient went to his psychiatrist and said "I'm concerned doctor. I keep having this dream that I'm a deck of cards." The doctor's reply? "Sit over there…I'll deal with you later."

*   *   *   *   *

A husband was upset because he had to spend so much time at the office, and didn't have enough time to take care of things at home. But then he heard about a new scientific procedure where he could be cloned.So he went for it. The man went to work, and the clone stayed home, taking care of things like mowing the lawn and so forth.

Unfortunately, clone technology was less then perfect, and this clone had a tendency to use really nasty language. One day, the clone was repairing the roof and started his usual swearing routine. The man's wife became totally fed up with the clone's constant cursing, so she snuck up behind him and pushed him off the roof. The clone fell to his death. The police soon arrived and gave the woman a $50 fine. Why so small? Well, the charge was only "making an obscene clone fall."

* * * * *

The name of Leif Ericson, the famous Viking explorer, was left off his town's new register. His wife was deeply upset, and complained to a local civic official, who apologized profusely and said, "I must have taken Leif off my census."

* * * * *

Mark Hamill played Luke Skywalker in the *Star Wars* trilogy and uttered the famous words "May the Force be with you!" He had a hard time finding acting work after playing that role, so he took a job teaching high school English. Now he says to his students, "Metaphors be with you!"

* * * * *

Charles Dickens was feeling despondent, because he couldn't come up with an idea for a new book. He didn't want to sit at home and mope, though, so he went to a nearby bar, where he ordered a martini. "Olive or twist?" asked the bartender.

* * * * *

Ever ask yourself if God cared about baseball? I think he must have, because the Bible starts with "In the big inning."

* * * * *

Here are a few questions and observations about some linguistic things that have been bugging me for a long time.

* When something doesn't work the way it's supposed to, we say it's "out of whack." What the heck is a "whack"?
* Are you as confused as me by the fact that "fat chance" and "slim chance" mean the same thing?
* Ditto with "slow down" and "slow up."
* Why do we usually sing "Take me out to the ball game" only when we're already there?
* Doesn't "after dark" really mean "after light"?
* Why are a "wise man" and a "wise guy" total opposites?
* How come the word "phonics" isn't spelled the way it sounds?

*   *   *   *   *

One night several years ago, when the Communists (often called "Reds") still had a firm grip on the Russian government, a couple was strolling down a Moscow street. The man felt something hit his nose.

"Darn! It's raining, dear," he said to his wife. "Oh, I think it's snow" she replied.

The bickering was off and running, but just before it got nasty, the couple spotted the head of the local chapter of the communist party walking toward them. "Let's ask Comrade Rudolph whether it's officially raining or snowing" the husband said. The wife agreed.

The couple made its way to Rudolph, and the husband asked "is it officially raining or snowing?" "It's raining, of course," Rudolph replied, and walked on.

"I told you" the man said to his wife.

"But that felt like snow," she declared.

To which the man calmly replied: "Rudolph the Red knows rain, dear."

* * * * *

Bud was in desperate need of some extra cash, so when his church announced it wanted to hire someone for the temporary job of painting its steeple, he applied for the position. And he got it.

He started the job about a week later, and quickly realized he could save himself a lot of money on paint if he just watered it down a bit. So he did. And he started painting again. After a little while, though, he was convinced the paint was still much thicker than he needed it to be. So he watered it down again. This went on a couple more times.

Bud started to paint the steeple a fifth time when a horrific storm struck. Thunder rolled, lightning lit up the sky, and rain poured. Bud's work disappeared completely.

Bud moaned rhetorically "Why did this happen?" A booming voice from the sky replied "Repaint, and thin no more!"

* * * * *

Did you read the news story saying that AT&T has put out a new line of personal phones made of seashells from beaches around the world? They're shellular phones.

* * * * *

A man was deeply upset because birds kept building nests in the mane of his horse. So he went to a vet and asked "What can I do to stop them?" "Just take some common yeast and sprinkle it in the horse's mane," the vet replied. "How would that help?" the man asked. The animal doc responded: "Because yeast is yeast and nest is nest and never the mane shall tweet!"

   *   *   *   *   *

Being an electrician can be really tough at times…you have to keep up with current events.

   *   *   *   *   *

A man was having mouth pain, so he went to his dentist. The tooth doc examined the man's mouth, and told him "I think I found the problem. That plate I put in last year has eroded." The patient was astonished that the deterioration had happened so fast, and said so. The dentist wasn't surprised, though, and asked the man if there were any particular foods he'd been eating a lot of over the past year. The man gave the question some quick thought, and then replied "Well, I got hitched a few months ago, and my wife makes this terrific hollandaise sauce. I put it on everything." The dentist frowned knowingly and said, "That's the problem. We'll have to put in a chrome plate." The man was confused and asked "Why chrome?" So the dentist answered: "Oh, there's no plate like chrome for the hollandaise!"

   *   *   *   *   *

A man had been on-line for eight hours, visiting his favorite web sites, collecting and answering e-mail, and playing computer games. His eyes had begun to hurt, but he stayed on-line.

"What are you doing now dear?," the man's concerned wife asked.

His reply? "I'm trying to find a site for sore eyes."

※　　　※　　　※　　　※　　　※

A newspaper reported that more than 250 hens were missing from a local chicken farm. Authorities suspected foul play.

※　　　※　　　※　　　※　　　※

Big dogs who lived in the hills surrounding Munich came down into the center of town and attacked everything in sight. The citizens of downtown Munich got together and drove the dogs back to the hills.

The dogs didn't give up though: they went over the hills to Leiden, which was well-known for its fine linen and had mills all over the place. The residents of Leiden didn't want to stay and fight the dogs, so they shut down the mills and left town. As the last citizen of Leiden was leaving, he heard some strange noises. So he turned around to take a look at what was going on. And he saw the dogs running into the linen mills, which were soon operating again. His conclusion? "The mills are alive with the hounds of Munich!"

Work Weirdness

◆

No doubt there are times when your job makes you want to throw in the towel. There are alternatives though—and laughing is a good one! Here's some humorous work-related material to help you do that.

*   *   *   *   *

I've seen and read about some truly bizarre notices on various products, and wondered what an employee was thinking when s/he wrote them. Here are just a few of the weirder ones I've run across.

- On a hairdryer: "Do not use while sleeping" (Darn—I like to dry my hair then).
- On a bar of soap: "Directions: Use like regular soap" (But I don't know how to do that!).
- On the box of a shower cap provided by a hotel: "Fits one head" (I guess two-headed guests have to call the front desk for a second cap).
- On packaging for an iron: "Do not iron clothes on body" (But wouldn't that save time?).
- On a children's cough medicine: "Do not drive car or operate machinery." (Amen to that! Just think of all the accidents we

could prevent if we kept sick 5-year-olds from driving cars and forklifts.)
* On a bottle of sleeping pills: "Warning: may cause drowsiness" (Thank goodness!).
* On a string of Chinese-made Christmas lights: "For indoor or outdoor use only." (There must be another "door" I never learned about).
* On a bag of peanuts: "Warning: contains nuts" (Those nutty peanuts!).
* On a packet of nuts provided by an airline: "Open packet, eat nuts" (Do I have to do it in that order?).

* * * * *

A business was looking for office help, and put a sign in its window that said:

"HELP WANTED. Applicants must be able to type, be good with a computer, and be bilingual." The sign ended with "We Are An Equal Opportunity Employer."

In short order, a dog walked up to the window and read the sign. He especially liked the part about the company being an equal opportunity employer. So he decided to apply for the position.

The dog got the receptionist's attention and pointed to the sign with his nose.

The receptionist figured out very quickly that the dog wanted to apply for the job. Unsure what to do about that, she summoned the office manager, who looked at the dog and was—to say the least—surprised. The dog seemed determined, though, so the manager led the pooch into the inner office. The dog jumped up on the chair and stared at the office manager, who said, "I'm sorry, but I can't hire you. As the sign says, you have to be able to type."

So the dog jumped down from his chair, headed to the typewriter, and typed a perfect letter at 90 words a minute. The dog then crossed the room, handed the letter to the officer manager, and went back to his chair.

The office manager was absolutely stunned. But he didn't want to hire a dog. So he told the canine applicant, "I can't give you the job. The sign says you have to be good with a computer."

That was no obstacle for the dog. He went to the computer and showed his expertise on it.

The manager was totally baffled again. But he looked at the dog and said "I still can't give you the job. As the sign says, the employee must be bilingual."

Without hesitating, the dog looked at the office manager and said: "Meow."

*   *   *   *   *

As I pointed out in a previous chapter, a lot of big names and scholars didn't exactly foresee the computer boom we've experienced over the past few years. The same sort of thing happened in the rest of the business world. Here are just a few of the more hysterical comments made by people and organizations that missed the business boat.

"Stocks have reached what looks like a permanently high plateau."
—Irving Fisher, Professor of Economics, Yale University, 1929

"Airplanes are interesting toys, but of no military value."
—Marechal Ferdinand Foch, Professor of Strategy, Ecole Superieure de Guerre.

"Everything that can be invented has been invented."

—Charles H. Duell, Commissioner, US Office of Patents, 1899

"This 'telephone' has too many shortcomings to be seriously considered as a means of communication. The device is inherently of no value to us."

—Western Union internal memo, 1876.

'The wireless music box has no imaginable commercial value. Who would pay for a message sent to nobody in particular?"

—David Sarnoff's associate's 1920's advice not to invest in the radio.

"A cookie store is a bad idea. Besides, the market research reports say America likes crispy cookies, not soft and chewy cookies like you make."

—A response to Debbie "Mrs. Fields."

"Who the hell wants to hear actors talk?"

—H.M. Warner, Warner Brothers, 1927.

"We don't like their sound, and guitar music is on the way out."

—Decca Recording Co. rejecting the Beatles in 1962.

"Heavier-than-air flying machines are impossible."

—Lord Kelvin, president, Royal Society, 1895.

* * * * *

Lots of people take an elevator to get to their offices. Elevator rides can be pretty dull, but here are some ideas on how to make them more interesting.

* While wearing a seriously pained look on your face, smack your forehead and scream "Shut up, dammit."
* Say "Ding!" at each floor.
* Whistle the first seven notes of "It's a Small World" over and over.
* Open your briefcase or purse just a little, peer inside, and say: "Got enough air in there?"
* Hand out name tags to everyone when they get on the elevator. Wear yours upside-down.
* When you arrive at your floor, make a big show of trying to open the doors: grunt, strain—the whole nine yards. Then act relieved and embarrassed when they open by themselves.
* Say "hello" to all the people getting on the elevator, shake their hands warmly, and ask them to call you "Captain."
* Choose one passenger, grin big-time at him/her for a while, and then announce "I'm wearing new socks!"
* Pick another passenger, and stare at him/her for a while. Adopt an amazed and frightened look, then announce "You're one of THEM!" and cower in a corner of the elevator.
* Meow repeatedly.
* Bet the other passengers you can fit a quarter in your nose—and then try to do it.
* Walk on carrying a cooler that says "human head" on the side.
* Wear a handpuppet and talk to the other passengers with it.

* When the elevator is silent, look around and ask someone "is that your beeper?"
* Say "I wonder what these do" loud enough for everyone on the elevator to hear you, and then push all the red buttons.
* Pull a stethoscope out of your bag or briefcase, put it on, and listen to the elevator walls with it.
* Draw a square on the floor around you with chalk. Inform the other passengers that this is your "personal space."
* Put some fear in the other passengers by announcing in a demonic voice "I must find a more suitable host body."
* Whenever anyone presses a button, make explosion noises.

* * * * *

Before I became a theater professor, I worked part-time as a waiter. I think that's a requirement for anyone interested in a career in the arts. I've also learned that going to a restuarant can be pretty dull for customers at times. If you want to make your restaurant time a little more interesting, though, here are five sure-fire ways to raise your server's blood pressure.

* Shout, "Sounds terrible!" every time s/he describes a special to you.
* Insist that before ordering the London broil, you must see and touch it.
* When the bill arrives, tie the tablecloth around your neck and say, "You wouldn't charge Superman for a meal, would you?"
* Eat the check.

* **And most important**—ask your server, "Are you a scary singer, awful artist, dreadful dancer, or atrocious actor?"

*　　*　　*　　*　　*

Sometimes you have to skip work for a day to preserve your sanity. These excuses might help.

* "Sorry, I can't come to work today. The voices in my head have told me to clean all my guns right away."
* "My stigmata's acting up."
* "I won't be at work today because I'll be stalking my previous boss, who fired me for not showing up one day."
* "I seem to have contracted some kind of attention-deficit disorder. It doesn't seem too serious, but…hey, how about them 'Skins?…So, I won't be in today…Hello, how can I help you?…I hope to be in tomorrow, though…Oh, I'll be sticking with Sprint, but thank you for calling."
* "I just found out that I was switched at birth. I really shouldn't come to work today since my employee records may contain false information."
* "I can't come to work today because my dog ate my car keys. We're going to hitchhike to the vet."
* "I won't be in today. My mother-in-law has come back from the dead, and my wife and I are going to drive a stake through her heart and give her eternal peace."

*　　*　　*　　*　　*

Lost in the translation? Sometimes your job requires you to travel to countries where English isn't the primary language. Foreign businesses know that many of their customers are English-speakers, though, and the attempts to meet the linguistic needs of these clients have led to some truly hysterical translations on their signs.

* In a hotel lobby: "The lift is being fixed for the next day. During that time we regret that you will be unbearable."
* On the menu at a restaurant: "Our wines leave you nothing to hope for."
* In an elevator: "Please leave your values at the front desk."
* At an airline ticket office: "We take your bags and send them in all directions."
* On a sign in a dress shop: "Ladies have fits upstairs."
* At a hotel desk: "If you consider our help impolite, you should see the manager."
* In an elevator: "Do not enter lift backwards, and only when lit up."
* On the door of a Moscow hotel room when there was still a U.S.S.R.: "If this is your first visit to the USSR, you are welcome to it."
* In the office of a doctor: "Specialist in women and other diseases."
* In a Tokyo shop: "Our nylons cost more than common, but you'll find they are best in the long run."
* In a cocktail lounge: "Ladies are requested not to have children in the bar."
* On the menu of a Polish hotel: "Salad a firm's own make; limpid red beet soup with cheesy dumplings in the form of a finger; roasted duck let loose; beef rashers beaten up in the country people's fashion."

* * * * *

There are times when work isn't too exciting. Here are four signs that you might be going through one of them:

* You stare at your cubicle wall over and over, and one time you do it so long you see an image of Elvis.
* You spend all sorts of work-time figuring out a way to get Gilligan off the island—even though the show's been off the air for years.
* Co-workers come into your office only to borrow pencils from your ceiling.
* The Paper Clip Division has overrun General White-Out's army and he's called the Staple Brigade for reinforcements.

* * * * *

You don't want to look bored, though, so here are a few helpful hints.

* Carry loads of stuff home with you at night—that will make your boss think you work a lot more than you actually do.
* Use a computer **a lot**. That will make you look really busy. In reality, though, a computer will allow you to send and receive personal e-mail, calculate your bonus, and generally kick back. When you get caught by your boss—and that **will** happen at some point—just say you're learning to use the new software he told you about, because you want to save the company some big bucks on training. There's another important benefit to using a computer: if you offer to show your boss what you learned, s/he will run away at approximately the speed of light.
* Keep your desk really messy. Clean desks are OK for top management, but for the rest of us, a clean desk just looks like we're not working hard enough. We're not talking a few spare papers, either. You should have huge piles of documents around your

workspace. More paper looks like more work. If you know that someone is coming to your cubicle, make the place look especially messy. Bury a paper you'll need about two feet down in a four-foot stack of "important documents." Make a big show of rummaging for it when s/he arrives.

* One really important part of the modern employment world is voice mail. You must never answer your phone—let your voice mail do it. You'll never get a call from a boss or co-worker who wants to give you something for free or do a job for you—they call because they want YOU to do something for THEM. So don't answer. Screen all your calls with voice mail. That way, if somebody leaves a voice mail message for you and it sounds like impending work, you can call back at lunch time, when almost no one is around. Then you can say you returned the call, but there was no answer. That way, you'll look like a responsible employee, and you can escape having to do any work. Your co-workers won't see you for the devious weasel you really are.

* Here's another great voice mail trick: if your voice mailbox has a limit on the number of messages it can hold, reach that limit all the time. It's easy to do. Just dial your work number repeatedly from home or the local bar, and leave yourself "earthshaking" messages, like weather reports or the latest sale items at the local discount store. Later callers will hear a recorded message that says something like, "Sorry, this mailbox is full"—which is "proof" you're a hard-working employee in high demand.

*   *   *   *   *

If your boss catches you sleeping in your cubicle, these excuses might help.

* "No sweat. I'm still billing the client."

* "They warned me at the blood bank this might happen."
* "I was just taking a 15-minute power-nap like they raved about in the time-management course you sent me to."
* "Sorry—I must have left the top off the liquid paper."
* "Actually, I wasn't sleeping. I was meditating on the company's mission statement and visualizing the success of a new paradigm."
* "Oh, I read that book you suggested to me, and this is one of the seven habits of highly effective people."
* "I was just testing my keyboard's drool-protection feature."
* "Actually, I was doing the 'Stress Level Elimination Exercise Plan.'" (abbreviated 'SLEEP')
* "I was just doing a Yoga exercise to help me overcome work related stress."
* "I wasn't sleeping. I was just trying to pick up my contact lens without using my hands."

*   *   *   *   *

Getting a job in the first place isn't a laughing matter. But the following real excerpts from cover letters and resumes definitely are.

* "I demand a salary commiserate with my extensive experience."
* "I have lurnt Word Perfect 6.0 computor and spreasheet programs."
* "Received a plague for Salesperson of the Year."
* "Wholly responsible for two (2) failed financial institutions."
* "Reason for leaving last job: maturity leave."
* "Failed bar exam with relatively high grades."

* "Let's meet, so you can 'ooh' and 'aah' over my experience."
* "I was working for my mom until she decided to move."
* "I have an excellent track record, although I am not a horse."
* "References: none. I've left a path of destruction behind me."
* "Finished eighth in my class of ten."
* "Instrumental in ruining entire operation for a Midwest chain store."
* "Marital status: often. Children: various."

About the Author

A former college theater professor and department chairman, Shawn Lovley was diagnosed with a brain tumor in April of 1987. Statistics say he was "supposed" to live five or six years after diagnosis. But his tumor was discovered more than a **dozen** years ago. Obviously, he's not a very good counter! Then again, maybe his love of laughter has helped him last. Deafened by the tumor, Shawn lives in the Maryland suburbs of D.eaf C.ity with his wife Magnificent Mary, a certified interpreter for the deaf, and their cool cats Hamlet and Tuxedo.

Made in the USA
Middletown, DE
21 March 2023